first time
EMBROIDERY AND CROSS-STITCH

Inspiring | Educating | Creating | Entertaining

Brimming with creative inspiration, how-to projects, and useful information to enrich your everyday life, Quarto Knows is a favorite destination for those pursuing their interests and passions. Visit our site and dig deeper with our books into your area of interest: Quarto Creates, Quarto Cooks, Quarto Homes, Quarto Lives, Quarto Drives, Quarto Explores, Quarto Gifts, or Quarto Kids.

First Published in 2019 by Quarry Books, an imprint of The Quarto Group,
100 Cummings Center, Suite 265-D, Beverly, MA 01915, USA.
T (978) 282-9590 F (978) 283-2742 QuartoKnows.com

Quarry Books titles are also available at discount for retail, wholesale, promotional, and bulk purchase. For details, contact the Special Sales Manager by email at specialsales@quarto.com or by mail at The Quarto Group, Attn: Special Sales Manager, 100 Cummings Center, Suite 265-D, Beverly, MA 01915, USA.

10 9 8 7 6 5 4

ISBN: 978-1-63159-797-8

Digital edition published in 2019

The content in this book appeared previously in *The Complete Photo Guide to Needlework* (CPi 2012) by Linda Wyszynski.

Library of Congress Cataloging-in-Publication Data available

Design and Page Layout: Megan Jones Design
Front Cover Image: shutterstock
Illustrations, graphs, and stitch photography: Dennis Wyszynski

Printed in China

first time

EMBROIDERY AND CROSS-STITCH

THE ABSOLUTE BEGINNER'S GUIDE

by Linda Wyszynski

QUARRY

contents

introduction

This book will open the door to the world of embroidery for you. There are always new threads, beads, and fabrics available that say, "come explore with me." Discover all the wonderful ways you can enjoy creating with stitches. Once you learn the stitches, anything is possible. Beautiful fabrics and threads are just waiting for you to pick them up and create.

There are no do's or don'ts in today's world of embroidery. We'll go over the equipment available, how to transfer designs, and how to start creating designs of your very own. You will find descriptions of different types of supplies that are available today. It is up to you to decide what you want to purchase. Some stitchers become collectors of tools, while others are attracted to threads, embellishments, or fabrics. You may be the stitcher who only purchases what is needed to complete the project at hand and then discovers your weakness along the way. I've never found my single weakness; I love it all.

We'll discuss different types of fabric that are suitable for the various techniques: creative embroidery, crewel, and cross-stitch. Once you learn the basic skills outlined for each technique, you'll be able to create any of the stitches found within those technique pages. A full-size photograph and a stitch graph will show in clear steps how the needle is to travel.

I often say keep the stitch straight or use the same height for each stitch. While this is important to follow if possible, it's also essential that you, as the stitcher, enjoy stitching. When my grandmother taught me to stitch when I was eight, it was important to her that each stitch be worked the best it could be. I was to remove the stitch and rework it if it wasn't perfect. Over the years I've tried—without success—to eliminate that reminder from my brain. Even today I hear Grandmother Coggins saying it could be a little straighter or the loops need to be the same height. Thanks to her I am able to create stitching works of art. But what your eye and hand create is a work of art each time you pick up a needle and thread—whether or not it is "perfect." Stitch for relaxation and have fun doing it!

In the pages of this book, you'll find all the information needed to get started. As you look over the projects, think about how you, as the stitcher, can complete a project as shown or be adventuresome and use the provided ideas but choose your own stitches, fabric, threads, and embellishments. Use the stitch guide sections as a resource when choosing new stitches or surfaces for the projects. Use whatever fabric, thread, or embellishment you fancy. The choice is yours to make.

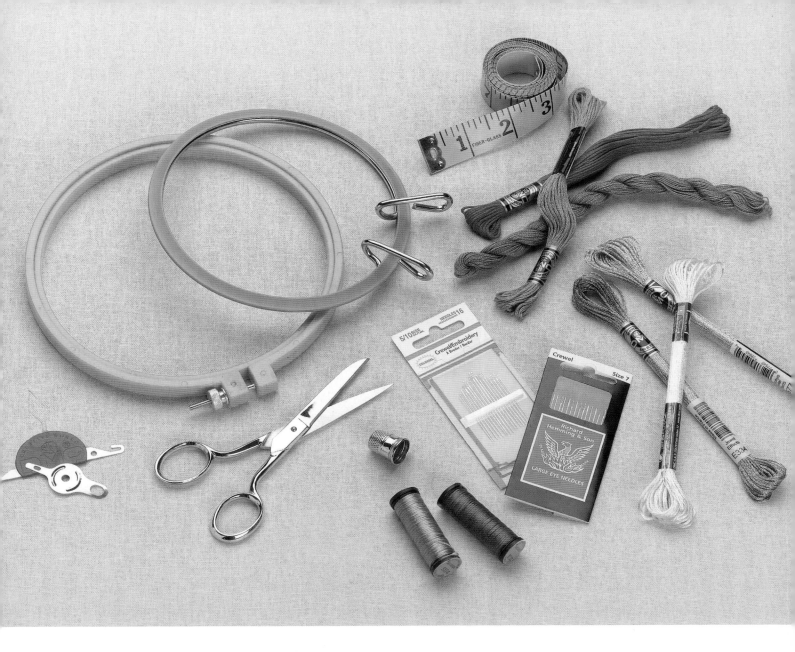

Get started by taking a shopping trip, and you will see the gorgeous colors of threads and fabrics along with the various tools that are available today. You only need a few basic supplies to create your first project. The world of embroidery is waiting for you to create whatever your imagination can conceive. Create a project using one or multiple techniques shown in this book. The ideas that come to mind are endless—from home décor to embellished jeans to jeweled cuffs. You are in the driver's seat for one of the wildest creative journeys of your life.

GETTING STARTED

×××××××××××××××××××××××××××××××××

All you need to get started is a needle, thread, fabric, pair of scissors, and an idea. The correct equipment enhances the embroidery experience and makes stitching much easier. Use the information in this section as a reference for choosing the correct equipment and supplies. You will refer to the information time and time again.

stitching equipment and supplies

Embroidery requires a very low investment in equipment and supplies, yet there are many options to consider. Many tools, fabrics, threads, and yarns can be used for more than one type of embroidery, and those items are introduced here.

NEEDLES

Needles are the most important tool required to create a beautiful piece of embroidered needle-work. The type and size of needle you choose depends on the fabric or canvas and the type of thread or wool to be used for the stitching.

A needle needs to fit your hand and feel comfortable when stitching. Choose a needle with an eye large enough for the thread or wool to move freely through but not larger than needed.

When you stitch, the threads of the fabric move, allowing the needle to slide through the weave. Once the needle passes through, those threads move back into place. But when you work with a needle that is too large, it leaves a hole in the fabric or enlarges the canvas hole.

Chenille Needles

Chenille needles are thick with large eyes and sharp points. Sizes range from 18 (largest) to 28 (smallest). Used for creative embroidery and crewel; the larger sizes are used for wool and crewel threads, size 3 and 5 pearl cotton, metallic braids, and silk ribbon. The smaller sizes are used for embroidery floss, over-dyed thread, combination threads (wool and silk), smaller sizes of metallic braids, and size 12 and 8 pearl cotton. Size 28 can be used for beading. This needle can be used on any fabric that has a plain-weave.

Crewel Needles

Crewel needles are thin with long eyes and sharp points. Sizes range from 1 (largest) to 10 (smallest). The larger sizes are used for wool and larger metallic braids. The smaller sizes are used for strands of cotton, silks, rayon thread, and smaller metallic braids. This needle can be used on any plain-weave fabric. Size 7 or 8 can be used for beading after the stitches are in place.

Embroidery Needles

Embroidery needles have long medium eyes and sharp points. Sizes range from 1 (largest) to 10 (smallest). They are used for creative embroidery and crewel, with stranded threads, silks, rayon, metallic thread, and braid. This needle can be used on any plain-weave fabric or for general hand sewing.

Milliners

Milliners are long and thin with very small eyes and sharp points. Sizes range from 1 (largest) to 10 (smallest). This needle is the same diameter down the length of the needle. Use a milliner to work a bullion knot that has a smooth even appearance. This needle can be used on any plain-weave fabric. It also works well for attaching beads with beading thread if a longer beading needle is not required.

These needles are excellent for finishing seams by hand or securing appliqués. The thin needle allows you to take small running stitches and to hide a slip stitch between the folds of fabric.

Sharps

Sharp needles are thin and short with small eyes and sharp points. Sizes range from 1 (largest) to 12 (smallest). These needles are excellent for finishing seams by hand or securing an appliqué. The thin needle allows you to take small running stitches and to hide a slip stitch between the folds of fabric.

Tapestry Needles

Tapestry needles are thick with large eyes and blunt points. They are slightly shorter than chenille needles and range in size from 18 (largest) to 28 (smallest). They are mainly used for cross-stitch and needlepoint and are perfect for working the whipped or laced portion of a crewel or creative embroidery stitch to prevent splitting the stitched thread. The larger sizes are used for wool, cotton thread, and crewel threads. The smaller sizes are used for embroidery floss, over-dyed, silk, and so on. Size 28 can be used for beading. This needle can be used on any even-weave fabric.

Chenille needles: Sizes 18, 22, and 26

Crewel needles: Sizes 1, 5, and 10

Embroidery needles: Sizes 5, 7, and 10

Milliners: Sizes 3, 7, and 10

Sharps: Sizes 6, 7, and 10

Tapestry needles: Sizes 18, 22, and 28

LOST NEEDLE

Keep a magnet handy to easily locate needles that fall on the carpet or into the chair. For safety's sake, always rescue the needle.

CUTTING TOOLS

Scissors or shears should be chosen for the task at hand. There are several types suitable for embroidery. To keep scissors or shears sharp, use them only for what they were designated. When scissors are not in use, they should be put away for safety. Keep scissors covered with a sheath or place them in the case they came in to protect the sharp point.

Embroidery scissors

Embroidery Scissors

Embroidery scissors are small and sharp and have a tapered point with a 1" (2.5 cm) blade cut. There are many different kinds available in a wide range of prices. These scissors are used to cut lengths of cotton, silk, or wool threads. When cutting thread lengths, it is recommended that you cut close to the base of the blade.

Fabric shears

Fabric Shears

Fabric shears are large and sharp and have a straight 8" (20.3 cm) blade. They are used for cutting all types of fabric.

STAY SHARP

Use older embroidery scissors for cutting synthetic fibers and metallic braids to keep your newer embroidery scissors sharp.

Paper Scissors or Shears

Paper scissors or shears are available in many sizes. Cut tissue paper and tape with these.

Cutting Board, Wide Ruler, and Rotary Cutter

This equipment is often thought of more for quilting than embroidery. Although they are not necessary for this type of stitching, these tools ensure clean, accurate cuts on all types of fabric. If you have a clean cut on the edge of your fabric, you have a well-finished project.

Paper scissors or shears

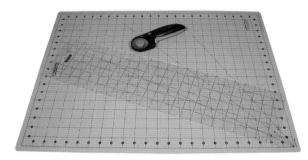

Cutting board, wide ruler, and rotary cutter

MULTIPLE SCISSORS

Use certain scissors or shears for specific items, so when you want a clean cut of thread or a smooth edge on the cut fabric you get what you expect. You do not need all the types of scissors discussed in this section to create a beautiful piece of embroidery.

HOOPS OR FRAMES

Creative embroidery, cross-stitch, and crewel are usually worked in a hoop or frame, though some stitchers prefer not to use them. Hoops and frames hold the work taut, making stitching easier and stitches more uniform. The size and type of hoop or frame will depend on the project and your preference. The following information will help you decide which type will work best for you.

When using a hoop, 2" to 3" (5.1 to 7.6 cm) of excess fabric should extend beyond the hoop or frame, before the fabric has been secured. This will help to keep the fabric taut once the hoop or frame has been tightened. When working on premade clothing, it is not always possible to have this much extra fabric. In such cases, you may find it easier to work the project without a hoop or frame.

If the hoop allows the fabric to slip during stitching, readjust the fabric as needed. When working on particularly delicate fabric, try wrapping the hoop with muslin fabric strips to lessen the stress on the fabric. Cut ½" (1.3 cm) strips of fabric to wrap around each of the hoop circles. Secure the end of the wrapped fabric with a small tack stitch.

Always remove the needlework from the hoop, clamp, or snap frame when not stitching. If they are left in place for longer than the stitching time, a permanent mark may develop on the fabric and thread. Or, frame up a larger piece of fabric than called for to keep the project area away from the frame or loop edges. This allows you to keep the fabric in the frame until the project is completed.

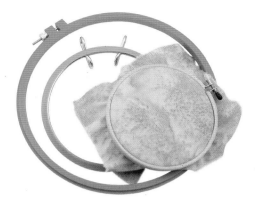

Wooden and plastic hoops

Wooden and Plastic Hoops

Wooden hoops have a screw tension. Plastic hoops come with a screw or spring tension. Both types of hoops have two round circles, one smaller than the other. To use a screw-tension hoop, separate the two circles and place the fabric over the smaller circle so it lies smoothly. Place the larger top circle over the fabric, pressing it into place. Gently screw the tension device to hold the work securely in place between the circles. The fabric needs to be taut across the bottom circle.

If using a hoop with a spring tension, be sure the fabric is smooth over the smaller circle before carefully placing the larger hoop on top. The spring-load tension will adjust automatically.

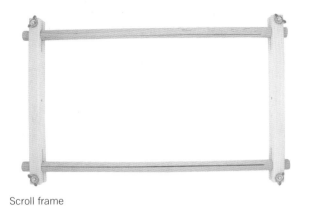

Scroll frame

Ratchet frame

Scroll Frame (with a split)

Slots in the dowel rods of this frame hold the fabric securely. You can adjust the tension so the fabric is taut for stitching. When you need to reposition the work, simply loosen the screws and roll to the desired area.

This type of frame makes it easy to quickly frame up and start the project without needing to tack or baste the work to the frame. It can be used for cross-stitch, crewel, and creative embroidery.

Ratchet Frame

This is a lightweight frame that works similarly to the wooden scroll frame. This system allows the fabric to scroll back and forth effortlessly on the two-way ratchets. The fabric is held at the correct tension between the two split rails without leaving marks on the fabric. Small or large projects can be worked on it without having to baste the fabric to the frame. The lightness of the frame makes it perfect for stitching and for traveling. It can be used when working cross-stitch, crewel, and creative embroidery.

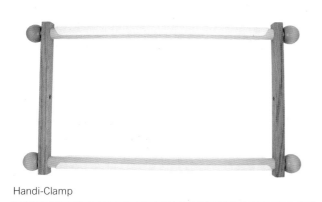

Handi-Clamp

Q-Snap frame

Handi-Clamp

This frame functions like the scroll frame, but it has two plastic clamps to hold the fabric in place. It does not require thumb tacks or staples and there is no basting. Simply lay the fabric over the dowel rod and snap the half-circular fastener in place on one end. Repeat for the other end. Use the knobs to roll up and tighten the fabric, making it taut in the frame. The company does recommend placing a piece of quilt batting (4" [10.2 cm] wide by the length of the scroll bar) between the frame and fabric to avoid marking the fabric with the frame bar. This frame is easy to use and is suitable for cross-stitch, crewel, and creative embroidery.

Q-Snap Frame

The Q-Snap is square. Place the fabric over the square and snap the half-circular fasteners in place on each side of the frame. Once the fasteners are in place, rotate them slightly away from you to tighten the fabric so it is taut in the frame. This frame works well for traveling.

KEEPING CLEAN

If you use a frame, slide your work into a pillowcase when you stop stitching to keep the work clean.

SUPPLIES

Beeswax

Available in needlework shops, beeswax is used to strengthen threads and reduce knotting or kinking. At times, you'll need a certain color of thread for beading. If you strengthen them with beeswax, you can use embroidery floss, hand-dyed single strand cotton, or sewing thread. Simply run the thread across the beeswax several times.

Iron and Ironing Board

It is important to remove all wrinkles from fabric before stitching. If fabric has been folded for long, lightly spray with water mixed with a teaspoon of white vinegar before light pressing. Batik fabric should be washed before spraying with vinegar water.

Press Cloth

This type of cloth is needed when fusing stabilizers to the wrong side of fabric. It is also handy when pressing a dark colored or synthetic fabric to avoid creating a shine on the fabric.

Light Source

Good lighting is important when stitching. Ideally, the light should come from over your shoulder. The best types of lighting are natural window light, daylight bulbs, and daylight fluorescent lamps.

Magnification

Several types of magnification work well. These include lighted floor stands, table lights with magnifiers, magnifiers that hang on a cord around the neck, and magnifiers that fit on your head allowing your glasses to remain in place.

My favorite is the magnifier that fits on your head. You can adjust it low enough to see the needlework while still being able to see above the top edge of the magnification. This allows you to watch TV or observe other people in the room.

Needle Threader

The needle and thread you choose will determine the kind of needle threader needed.

Magnification

Beeswax

Needle threader

Quilter's Tape

This is a tape with a light adhesive that will not leave a residue on fabric. Use it to hold tissue paper on the right side of the fabric until basting it in place. Mark the tape every ¼" or ½" (0.6 or 1.3 cm) to help keep your border stitches evenly spaced. Remove the tape when you're done stitching for the day—do not leave tape on the fabric for more than a few hours. Read all product instructions before using.

Quilter's tape

Ruler and Measuring Tape

Keep a measuring tape handy to locate the center of your fabric before placing your design. A small ruler is handy for measuring the length of a stitch or for accurately placing patterns.

Ruler and measuring tape

Laying Tool or Stiletto

Either of these tools can be used to lay a metal thread or stranded thread so it does not twist as it enters the canvas. When these tools are not in use, secure the stiletto tip or place the laying tool in its case. Store this tool out of the reach of children.

Laying tool or stiletto

Straight Pins and Pin Cushion

Use straight pins to hold fabrics together or to mark a starting point on canvas or stitchery. Straight pins can be used to straighten out a knot in your thread. If you have a kink in a creative embroidery thread that doesn't want to lie smoothly against the fabric, just use the pin as a laying tool.

Thimbles

Using a thimble is entirely optional. When used, it is normally worn on the middle finger to help push the needle through heavier fabrics. You may find the feel of a thimble awkward at first. It will take time to learn to stitch using one, but it prevents pricking a finger.

Thimbles

Magnets

Placing a magnet on each side of your fabric creates the perfect spot to place your needle while stitching.

Magnets

Tweezers

These little jewels are a must in every needle-work basket. They help to remove threads that have been clipped, extract bits of tissue paper that are stuck under a stitch, and pick up a needle that is buried deep in the carpet.

Tweezers

fabrics

When planning your project, choose a fabric suited to the pattern and finished design. Use a fabric that will showcase your thread colors when the project is finished.

There is a wide range of fabrics, clothing, kitchen items, and even paper that can be embroidered. Fabric that has give, or stretches, does not work well. The thread does not stretch, causing the fabric to pucker. Use a stabilizer like medium-weight Pellon, or two layers of fabric if cotton is being used. A lightweight flannel also works well.

Crewel work is usually done with heavy thread, and heavyweight fabrics work well. Linen fabric can also be used.

There is an endless range of cross-stitch fabric and premade items available for cross-stitch. High-count linens worked over several threads result in a beautiful finished project. Waste canvas is available to attach to regular fabric or clothing items.

FABRIC PREPARATION

Before using washable fabric, wash, dry, and iron fabric following the manufacturer's instructions. If you do not prewash the fabric, it may shrink when it is washed later, distorting the stitches.

If your finished project will not be washed, it is not necessary to prewash the fabric. Washing removes sizings, which are used in some fabrics to give the fabric a crisp look that enhances the finished project.

When using a loosely woven fabric, overcast (zigzag) the edges. Some stitchers prefer to always overcast or serge the edges or run a quick basting hem along the edges.

If you find a fabric you like that isn't included here, ask for a small sample of it to work a few stitches on. Then answer the following questions to determine if the fabric is suitable for the stitching technique. Did the needle slide easily in and out of the fabric? Did the fabric lay flat after the stitches were in place? Do you like the effect of the stitches and thread with the fabric?

COTTONS (PLAIN-WEAVE)

Cotton fabrics are available in an array of beautiful, lush solid colors. The batiks make a wonderful background for embroidery. They come in a wide range of colors, including multicolored.

White-on-white and cream-on-cream prints or stripes (patterns on the fabric are of like color) give just a hint of texture to the background for embroidering. In the quilting world, this type of fabric is used for the quilt pattern background. I love stitching on this type of white fabric. The threads bring the color to the project.

Muslin—unbleached or bleached white— is a lightweight fabric. It comes in 100 percent cotton or a 50/50 blend. The 100 percent cotton is a good choice for embroidery. Available in different thread counts (a higher thread count works best), it is a nice surface for kitchen towels, aprons, and pillows. Muslin also works well with transfer paper, window tracing, or iron-on pencil.

Good for: creative embroidery

QUILTING COTTON

Cotton works well for crewel projects. This fabric comes in wonderful colors. Kona cotton is a little thicker than other brands on the market, making it a favorite. Do use a stabilizer with cotton.

Good for: crewel

SHEER

This transparent fabric is slippery and can be a little difficult to work with. Layer two pieces together to create a little more weight to the fabric. You can choose a darker tone of the same color, or use a contrasting color under the sheer. Adding a piece of stabilizer under the solid fabric would give the two pieces of fabric even more

stability. This fabric is beautiful when used by itself or in combination with a piece of solid colored fabric. It is well worth the effort once the project is complete.

Good for: creative embroidery

SILK NOIL

This natural silk has a nubby texture that enhances your stitchery. Wonderful for purses or picture frames, the fabric comes in a wide range of colors. Black or off-white colors are wonderful backgrounds for colorful stitchery.

Good for: creative embroidery

SHANTUNG

This shiny fabric has crosswise ribs and slubs, giving character and texture to the fabric. It works especially well for home décor projects. Shantung has a fine texture and is woven from cultivated silk. There is also a synthetic fabric that looks like shantung. It is hard to tell the difference between the two. The synthetic is a slightly lighter fabric. Both types work but need to be stabilized.

Good for: creative embroidery and crewel

FELT

Felt comes in wool blends, bamboo, and 100 percent wool. The wool blends and bamboo are widely available, and the 100 percent wool can be found in specialty shops or online. Felt is easy to use and does not ravel. Projects can quickly be finished by using one of the edging stitches.

Good for: creative embroidery and crewel

LINEN

Linen fabric found in fabric stores comes in several colors along with a natural color that is sold in the home décor area. The natural color is thinner than linen found in needlework shops. It can be used with a stabilizer. Even-weave linens from needlework shops can be used for crewel. The higher count linens work best for this technique. Loosely woven linens (gaps between threads) do not work well. The stitches will slide under the threads. The higher the fabric count, the easier it is to work the stitches. Glasgow linen is a slightly heavier linen. It works well with wool or blends.

Good for: creative embroidery, crewel, and cross-stitch

UPHOLSTERY OR DRAPERY WEIGHT

There are stunning fabrics to be found in the home décor area of large fabric stores. I recently found a herringbone weave for upholstery that I am looking forward to using. Patterned, striped, textured, and silky fabrics work well for this technique. The type of fabric you choose to use will depend on the design and threads being used.

Good for: crewel

DUPIONI

This interesting silk has a tight weave with irregular crosswise slubbed yarns that form ribs across the fabric. It is a light- to medium-weight fabric with a rough texture and dull sheen. It comes in natural or bleached white as well as bright dyed colors. This is a favorite choice for many crewel stitchers. The natural colored silk is beautiful when stitched using wool, silk, and cotton threads. The textures of the fabric and threads give the design an added elegance.

Good for: crewel

CORDUROY

This fabric comes with a wide wale and fine wale. The wale gives the fabric a ribbed look that can add interest to the stitching. Choose the size wale that fits with the design you are stitching. A smaller detailed design would work better on a fine wale. For the wide wale, Persian yarn and pearl cottons work well. This is a seasonal fabric that is usually found in fabric stores in the fall.

Good for: crewel

HAND OVER-DYED WOOL

This fabric comes in stunning over-dyed colors with the shades of color flowing over the wool fabric. Wool fabric with wool thread mixed with silks and single-strand cotton give an interesting textured look to any design. Wool does not ravel and can be finished with edging stitches.

Good for: crewel

OVER-DYED FABRIC

Aida, linen, metallic, and specialty-weave fabrics all come in over-dyed varieties. There is a large range of counts and colors in these fabrics. Aida comes in 11 to 20 count. Linen comes in 28 to 40 count and the Specialty-Weave 10 count Tula. More colors and types of over-dyed fabric are becoming available all the time, as cross-stitchers love working on them.

Good for: cross-stitch

AIDA AND AIDA BLENDS

Aida is available in count sizes from 8 to 18. It comes in 100 percent cotton and cotton blends. The 100 percent cotton is a stiff fabric, making it easier to stitch. After stitching, Aida fabric can be washed and pressed and it becomes much softer. The most popular size is 14 count, which is currently available in over five dozen colors. The color wheel is represented well with all the available colors.

There are different kinds of Aida—the metallic collection, country, homespun, and vintage to name a few. These are made from 100 percent cotton or cotton blended with rayon, polyester, or linen.

Good for: cross-stitch

SPECIALTY WEAVE FABRICS

These blended fabrics are manufactured using a combination of two of the following types of threads: cotton, rayon, linen, and metallic. The count ranges from 7 to 28. Two higher count fabrics that are easy to work on are Tula (rayon and cotton) in 10 count and Klostern (rayon and cotton) in 7 count. Jute (100 percent Jute) in 12 count is wonderful for country-style projects. Cross-stitch metallic fabric has flecks of gold or silver sprinkled over the cloth. These flecks of gold and silver add interest to certain types of designs.

Good for: cross-stitch

threads

When choosing thread for a project, consider what the project will be used for. Choose a thread that can be washed if the project will require it. Most thread today can be washed by hand, while others need to be dry-cleaned.

When purchasing over-dyed, hand-dyed, and variegated threads, buy the full quantity the project requires at the same time, and be sure that all of the threads are from the same dye lot; threads from a different dye lot may vary slightly in color. Even silks and stranded cotton could have a slight difference in color, although the difference is not usually noticeable on a project. These threads do not list a dye lot on the package. A very slight difference would only be detectable if stitching a large background with one color. If you are working such a project and find you are running short on thread, stop stitching and purchase the new thread. Then alternate cut strands from each of the skeins of thread to blend the new color with the previous color.

PEARL COTTON (COTON PERLÉ)

This cotton thread is slightly twisted and is used as a single strand. It has a beautiful sheen with many colors to choose from along with several sizes. Sizes used for creative embroidery are 5, 8, and 12. Size 12 is used for very fine work, and 5 can be used as a laid thread for couching. Sizes 12, 8, and 5 can be used for cross-stitch on Aida and linen. When working with pearl cotton, the section of thread that is in the eye of the needle loses its sheen and becomes dull. Avoid using this section for working stitches.

Good for: creative embroidery, cross-stitch

SIX-STRAND EMBROIDERY FLOSS

Made with 100 percent cotton, this six-strand embroidery floss thread is available in solid and variegated colors. There is a large range of solid colors to choose from and many of these colors come in a range of shaded tones. Cotton threads are very versatile and easy to use. You will need to watch your tension when stitching with cotton, as there is no stretch or give to the thread.

Good for: creative embroidery, crewel, cross-stitch

LINEN

There are several 100 percent linen threads available. These textured threads come in six strand and a single strand. The strands vary in width along the strand. It is easy to work with, although the strands have a slightly coarse texture. There is a wide range of colors. Dye lots vary, so it's best to purchase the amount needed.

Good for: creative embroidery, cross-stitch

SATIN AND RAYON

These six-strand threads have a very silky, shiny sheen. They work best for flat, straight stitches or satin stitches but can also be used in place of stranded cotton with careful manipulation. Although they are slippery to work with, these threads are well worth the effort when the end result is viewed. These threads are manmade but contain some natural fiber so they do not fall into the synthetic thread range.

Good for: creative embroidery

SYNTHETIC THREAD

These polyester threads are beautiful when stitched. Varieties include tubular threads that have a nice shiny appearance and work well for flat laid stitches to be couched down. There is also a single-strand thread that has a slight twist in the thread with a metallic fleck embedded along the thread. This thread works well for projects where just a little bit of sparkle is desired.

Good for: creative embroidery

COTTON HAND-DYED AND OVER-DYED

These threads come in a skein in six-strand embroidery floss and a single-strand thread. They are a joy to work with and are especially appropriate when filling an area. Once a pattern is worked with these threads, there can never be another exactly like it. The dyes create lovely shades of color along the thread. Use the thread as it comes from the skein. Knot the end of the thread that was previously cut before cutting a new length. By using the previous cut to begin stitching, you will match the color range of the thread you just ended.

Good for: creative embroidery, crewel, cross-stitch

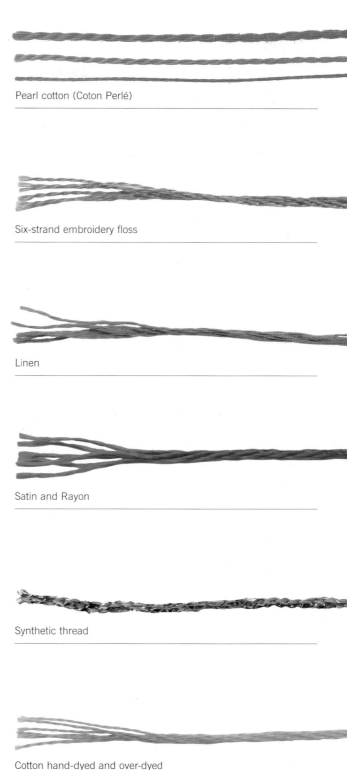

Pearl cotton (Coton Perlé)

Six-strand embroidery floss

Linen

Satin and Rayon

Synthetic thread

Cotton hand-dyed and over-dyed

SILK

Silk comes in hand-dyed and solid colors, and is easy to stitch with. It is available on a spool in a six- or twelve-stranded thread, a single-thread card or skein, and in half skeins. It has a soft sheen, adding beauty to a design.

Silk also comes with metallic flecks scattered along the thread to give just a touch of bling to the stitches. This silk has a look of its own and is a very soft thread. The added metallic is a thread that is woven into the twisted strands. To see how it looks stitched, check out the fedora hat band project on page 101.

Good for: creative embroidery, crewel, cross-stitch

BRAID (METALLIC)

This metallic braid comes on a spool in many sizes. The very fine size 4 braid, fine size 8 braid, and tapestry size 12 braid work best for creative embroidery and crewel. The larger size 12 braid is great for using as a thread to couch over or for straight stitches where a touch of metallic is desired. For cross-stitch, size 4, 8, and 12 also work best for even-weave fabric. This braid should have a little space in the corner it comes up and goes down in. Using a braid that is too large for the thread count will take away from the beauty of the braid. It should lie flat against the fabric. This twisted braid is a dream to stitch with and a great way to add a little sparkle to your project. It is very flexible, which makes it ideal for working curved lines, and it can be used for any type of stitch.

Good for: creative embroidery, crewel, cross-stitch

STRANDED METALLIC

Stranded metallic can be used as a single strand or in combination with floss. If you would like a little sparkle but not the full effect of metallic, you can use one strand of floss and one strand of metallic. It is a bit slippery, so watch your tension.

Good for: creative embroidery, crewel

MEMORY THREAD

This thread—which is really a flexible copper wire wrapped with a soft fiber—adds a dimensional appearance to a design. It works well on fabric or paper. Memory thread is wonderful for decorative stitches and embellishing. You can use it as a laid stitch to be couched.

When using as a laid stitch, place a couching stitch over the ends to hold the wrapped fiber on the wire in place. Memory thread can be used for basket handles, flower stems, butterfly wings, and coiled for flower centers. When working antennae on the butterfly you can use memory thread. If you want a coil, simply wrap the thread around a large needle. The bendable thread will allow you to secure one end of the length and leave the other end so it is slightly elevated above the fabric.

Good for: creative embroidery, cross-stitch

CREWEL WOOL

This 100 percent wool yarn is single-strand soft wool. It is two strands twisted together to create one strand of wool and should not be separated. To work most crewel stitches, you will need to join several strands of this wool. The number of strands used depends on how thick a stitch you want for the area you are filling. This wool comes in a wide range of colors.

Good for: crewel

TIP When stitching with wool or wool-blend yarns, leave a little more space between stitches than when working with a finer thread. You want the thread, or wool, to lie flat and smooth against the fabric.

Silk

Braid (Metallic)

Stranded metallic

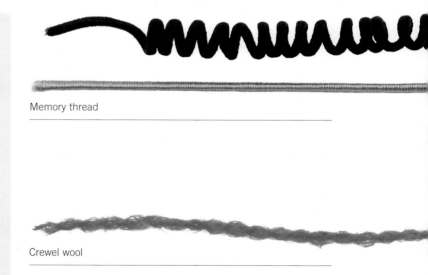

Memory thread

Crewel wool

BLENDING THREADS

Looking for ways to blend thread for different effects?

✄ Use one strand of a non-metallic thread with a strand of metallic to create a little glitz. When working the blended stitches, the metallic may not show on every stitch, adding further interest to the area.

✄ Use one strand of a cotton thread with a strand of over-dyed or hand-dyed to add a touch of additional color to an area. Create a subtle look to an area of stitching by using a light and a dark shade of solid color threads with the same number of strands.

PERSIAN YARN

This 100 percent virgin wool yarn is a three-ply yarn. You will need to separate the strands before stitching. It can be purchased in hanks, skeins, or by the pound. Some needlework shops also sell it by the three-ply strand. It comes in 230 shaded colors. Stitching with this yarn creates a slightly fuzzy appearance, adding an interesting texture to the stitched area.

Good for: crewel

Persian yarn

WOOL BLENDS

These blends come in single strand or three ply in fiber blends of wool/acrylic and wool/silk. The single-strand wool/silk blend is very easy to work with and seems to glide in and out of the fabric effortlessly.

Good for: crewel

Wool blends

HAND OVER-DYED STRANDED COTTON

This is a six-strand cotton that can be used for couching, lacing stitches, French knots, and feather stitches. This thread has a soft blending of color that runs along the thread. It can add a touch of shading when working shapes or filling in areas.

Good for: crewel

Hand over-dyed stranded cotton

TWISTED HAND-DYED COTTON

This three-ply pima cotton thread comes in beautiful variegated hand-dyed colors. The variegated colors of this twisted thread give your stitches beautiful color flowing across the fabric. One strand can be used for crewel work, and the three-ply strand (do not separate) can be used as a laid thread to couch over. You'll need to separate the plies of thread (page 38) before using for cross-stitch. One ply can be used on 11–20 count depending on your choice of fabric. For some linen fabric, two-ply thread may be necessary. Dye lots vary so it's best to purchase the amount needed.

Good for: crewel, cross-stitch

Twisted hand-dyed cotton

SPECIALTY THREAD

This single-strand polyester with metallic flecks along the thread comes in many colors. It is easy to work with and can be used on fabric that is not as tightly woven. It works well on linen and silks.

Good for: crewel

Specialty thread

CONVERSION CHARTS

If you like the colors in a pattern but would like to change the thread type, there are conversion charts available to assist you. Thread companies provide conversion charts so you can reference a six-stranded floss color and find out which single-strand thread is closest in color. There are also conversion charts for silk to floss. Look for these and other conversion charts on the Internet. Most thread companies allow you to print their conversion charts.

charts, diagrams, and patterns

DESIGN CHARTS

Cross-stitch is worked from a chart and is referred to as counted work. Creative embroidery and crewel are normally considered free-form techniques. If worked using a chart and even-weave fabric, they then become counted work. The creative embroidery and crewel techniques are shown in a free-form style in this book, which allows more freedom when working the stitches.

CROSS-STITCH CHARTS

Cross-stitch charts are shown on a square grid. Each stitch is represented by a square on the chart. The color key and chart have corresponding symbols that indicate the color, type of thread, and amount of thread needed for each stitch. Information is given if the cross-stitch is worked over one or two threads on even-weave fabric. Some patterns give sizes of the design when worked on more than one type of fabric and fabric count. Others indicate the fabric size needed for that project. When counting cross-stitch, count each square on the pattern for correct placement on the fabric. For more information refer to the Cross-Stitch chapter (page 107).

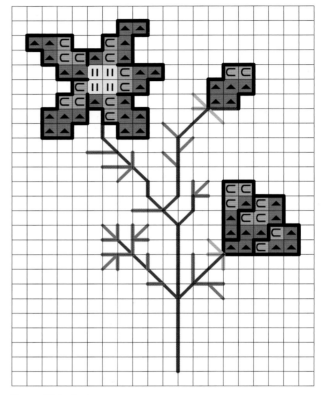

Cross-stitch chart

STITCH DIAGRAMS

Cross-stitch and needlepoint have diagrams that show a grid line with arrows and/or numbers to indicate where to place the stitch. Creative embroidery and crewel have diagrams that show how the stitch is worked without a grid. These diagrams have arrows and numbers, but the stitch length is up to the stitcher.

DESIGN PATTERNS

Patterns for creative embroidery and crewel come in the form of line drawings, pattern books, kits, and stamped pattern packs. For the line drawings and pattern books, you'll need to transfer the pattern onto the fabric to be used. This information is discussed under Transferring Patterns (page 32). Stamped patterns are purchased in pattern packs and come in a wide range of themes. The stamped design is ironed directly to the fabric. Follow the manufacturer's instructions to transfer the pattern onto the fabric.

Hand drawings are really patterns that you can transfer using any of the methods discussed in this section. Create a keepsake for your child by turning one of their drawings into a finished piece of needlework.

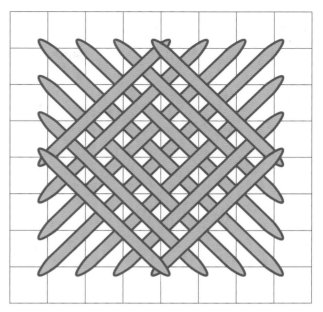

Needlepoint stitch

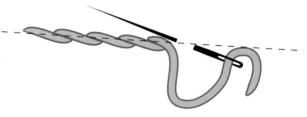

Embroidery diagram

Line drawing

Drawing by Rileigh Pack, age 11

transferring patterns and stabilizing fabric

Once you have the design and fabric, you will need to decide how to transfer the design to the fabric and how to stabilize the fabric, if necessary. The subjects of design transfer and stabilizers are closely related.

There are several ways to transfer an original design or pattern to your fabric. The fabric and stabilizer used often determines which transfer method to use. With a little experimentation, you will soon decide the type of transfer method and supplies you prefer. I use the basting method with tissue paper or the non-fusible stabilizer more than any other method. I like the transfer results of the basting.

TRACING

Tracing is a key technique when transferring designs. There are many considerations when selecting an appropriate marker or pencil for use when tracing.

Permanent or Waterproof Pens

Use these pens to trace the pattern onto the stabilizer or tissue paper. Once the pattern is traced, it's best to let the ink dry for a few minutes before placing it next to the fabric and basting the design. These two types of pens should not rub off on the thread or ribbon when the stitches pass through the traced area.

Here are some examples of pens: Pigma Micron black fine pen, which is a micro pigment ink waterproof pen purchased in art stores, and Sharpie permanent black fine pen available in drug stores, discount stores, and so on. Be sure the Sharpie says that it is permanent. Do not use either of these types of pen directly on fabric because the lines will not come out when the fabric is washed.

Pencils

A mechanical, #4 hard, or marking pencil can be used to trace the pattern onto the stabilizer or tissue paper. If using white or very light colored threads, ribbons, or silk, the pencil lead could leave a slight discoloration on the threads or fabric surface. Most pencil lines marked directly on fabric will come out when washed, but there is always the chance they will remain visible.

Vanishing or Water-erasable Marking Pens

These widely available pens can be used to draw a pattern directly onto the fabric. They work especially well for children, who can draw their own pattern and then execute the stitches of their choice. If using the water-erasable pen, be sure to wash the project after the stitching is completed to remove the marked lines. The vanishing pen lines should indeed simply vanish. Follow the product directions carefully. Also, try to keep fabric marked with these pens out of the direct sun, as heat could set the marks permanently.

Tracing on Fabric Method

Use a sunny window or light box to trace directly onto the fabric. Place the fabric over the pattern, centering the pattern in the correct position. Pin the pattern to the fabric. Recheck placement by holding the fabric up to the sunny window or placing it on the light box. When you are satisfied with the placement, tape the fabric to the light box or window, using ¼" (6 mm) quilter's tape. Trace the pattern using an appropriate marker or pencil. This is a quick and easy way to transfer the pattern.

Vanishing or water-erasable Marking Pens

Tracing on fabric

SMALL DETAILS

When tracing a design that has small details like embellished beads or small lazy daisies, use a straight line or small dot to indicate where they are to be placed. Every mark you make on the fabric must be covered with a stitch or it will show. For beads used for embellishment, rather than indicate it on the transfer, use the pattern as a guide for placement.

Tracing Using Transfer Paper and Stylus Method

This method uses colored tracing or transfer papers to trace the pattern directly onto the fabric. The papers are available in several colors, and the color should not smear or come off on the thread. If the pattern has writing on the back, trace the pattern onto tracing paper or tissue paper before transferring it to fabric or stabilizer. Simply place the traced pattern in correct position over the fabric. Slip the transfer paper under the design, carbon against the fabric. Use the stylus as you would a pencil, bearing down on the stylus with a little pressure. Trace over the pattern, transferring it to the fabric.

These are some of the transfer papers available: DMC wax-free tracing paper that is less powdery than others on the market. It will wash out. Clover's tracing paper does not smear, and it will wash out, but it does transfer a stronger color to the fabric. This paper comes in brighter colors. Loew Cornell transfer paper is greaseless, wax-free, erasable, and smudge-proof. It's best to test the product on a scrap of fabric to be sure you like the results before using it on your project fabric. Always read the product instructions.

IRONING METHOD

Heat Transfer Pencil

Heat transfer pencils, available in craft and fabric stores, allow you to transfer patterns directly to the fabric. The lines are permanent, so they should only be used if the needlework will cover the lines entirely. This method transfers the mirror image of the pattern, so trace the pattern onto tissue paper first using plain pen or pencil, then flip the paper over and trace the lines with the heat transfer pencil. Center the pattern facedown on the right side of the fabric, and pin in place. Transfer the pattern to the fabric with a heated iron, following the pencil manufacturer's directions.

Transfer paper

Heat transfer pencil

Basting through tissue paper on right side

BASTING METHOD

With this method, the pattern is transferred to stabilizer or tissue paper before basting it onto the fabric. The basted stitches remain on the fabric until you stitch over them or remove them. They will not disappear, require washing, or discolor the fabric or threads. This method gives you the truest transfer. Although it does require a few more minutes to baste the pattern onto the fabric, the results are well worth it, especially when transferring larger patterns.

To baste the pattern in place, use either sewing thread or one strand of embroidery floss that matches the colors of threads to be used to complete the pattern. For ease in removing basting thread, do not knot ends. Instead, take two small backstitches to begin and end the basting thread. When the stitching of the project is completed, remove any basting threads that show. As you stitch the project, you will cover most, if not all, of the basting stitches, saving you the extra time it would take to remove them.

Basting Using Tissue Paper

This method works well for all types of projects, especially for small designs on clothing. Use a low-temperature iron to press out any wrinkles in the paper. Trace the pattern onto the tissue paper using a fine-tip black permanent pen or pencil. Then center the traced pattern faceup on the right side of the fabric, and pin in place. Baste the pattern onto the fabric, stitching through the tissue paper and fabric. When the entire pattern has been basted, run the tip of the needle along the basting lines to score the tissue paper; then carefully tear the paper away. Use tweezers to remove any little pieces of tissue paper that remain.

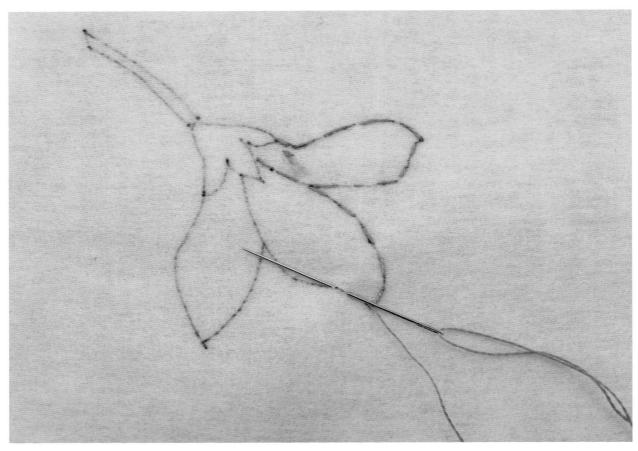

Basting through stabilizer on wrong side

Basting Using Fusible Stabilizer

This method works well for medium-weight fabrics like corduroy, twill, and home décor items. Be sure your fabric choice can withstand the temperature required for fusing. Pellon's feather-weight fusible stabilizer is a good choice. Using an appropriate marker or pencil, trace the pattern onto the stabilizer. Then center the traced pattern facedown on the wrong side of the fabric, and pin in place. The pattern can easily be seen through the stabilizer. Fuse the stabilizer to the fabric, following the manufacturer's instructions, and allow to cool. Working from the wrong side, baste the pattern onto the right side, stitching thorough the stabilizer and fabric so the pattern shows clearly on the right side.

SMALL DESIGNS

If stitching a small area on clothing, baste close to the tissue pattern to secure it to the fabric. Then bypass the basting step and work the decorative stitches through the tissue paper onto the fabric. This does not work well for large areas because the tissue paper will tear and the pattern will be unusable.

Basting Using Non-Fusible Stabilizer

This method works well for light- to medium-weight opaque home décor and clothing items. Pellon #30 non-fusible stabilizer is easy to use and gives the finished work a little body. Using an appropriate marker or pencil, trace the pattern onto the stabilizer. Then center the traced pattern facedown on the wrong side of the fabric, and pin in place. The pattern can easily be seen through the stabilizer. Working from the wrong side, baste the pattern onto the right side, stitching thorough the stabilizer and fabric so the pattern shows clearly on the right side. For clothing, trim away excess stabilizer after the needlework is finished.

OTHER STABILIZERS

The following stabilizers are opaque, making it necessary to use one of the transferring methods that transfer to the front of the fabric. Suggestions include: Basting Using Tissue Paper, Heat Transfer Pencil, and Tracing Using Transfer Paper and Stylus.

Fusible Fleece (Pellon)

Fusible fleece works well to stabilize lighter-weight fabric. It does require that you transfer the pattern using one of the transfer methods discussed in this chapter.

The fleece gives body to the fabric while adding padding between the fabric and the back of the work. It helps to keep the fabric from wrinkling. The downside of the product is that it can leave small bits of batting on the front of the fabric if stitches need to be removed. This product works well with creative embroidery and crewel.

STRAIGHT LINES

Baste a guideline or place a piece of quilter's tape straight across the area to be stitched on the plain-weave fabric. Measure from the bottom edge of the fabric up to the guide to be sure it is straight.

stitching basics

FABRIC PREPARATION

Before using washable fabric for creative embroidery, crewel, and cross-stitch, wash, dry, and iron fabric following the manufacturer's instructions. If you do not prewash the fabric, it may shrink when it is washed later, distorting the stitches.

If your finished project will not be washed, it is not necessary to prewash the fabric. Washing removes sizings, which are used in some fabrics to give the fabric a crisp look that enhances the finished project.

When using a loosely woven fabric, overcast (zigzag) the edges. Some stitchers prefer to always overcast or serge the edges or run a quick basting hem along the edges.

THREAD DETAILS

For easy stitching, thread should be cut in 14" to 16" (35.6 to 40.6 cm) lengths for stitching. Metallic thread and braids should be cut in 12" to 14" (30.5 to 35.6 cm) lengths. Some types of thread and most yarn (even strand cotton) become fuzzy if the length is longer than 16" (40.6 cm).

The nature of thread is to become twisted as you stitch. To counter this, form a habit of twisting your needle clockwise one turn after every few stitches to keep the thread straight. You can also let the needle and thread dangle downward from the fabric to allow the thread to untwist.

Some thread manufacturers indicate how many strands to use for the different sizes of even-weave fabric. There are so many threads on the market, it is impossible to list them all and give the number of strands to use for each fabric count. You will need to determine if the thread is covering the canvas, plain-weave, or even-weave fabric. Some stitchers prefer a heavy thread look

to their needlework while others like a lighter look. See which look you like best.

Stranded Thread

All threads that are stranded should be separated and then plied back together unless otherwise noted in a pattern. This gives you better coverage when stitching. Hold the cut length between your thumb and index finger, leaving a small amount of thread exposed above the fingers. Separate one strand from the rest and pull that thread straight up. Continue until the number of strands needed have been separated. Use the number of strands called for by putting the plies back together.

Braids (Metallic)

Stitching braids come on spools. When you cut a length, it likes to slightly curl. To smooth out the thread, simply run your fingernail down the cut length.

SILKY FLOSS

Six-strand embroidery floss and stranded satin thread take on a more silky look and are easier to handle when they have been dampened and dried. Cut strands 14" to 16" (35.6 to 40.6 cm) long, and run them one at a time over a slightly damp sponge. Lay the dampened threads aside to dry (some colors will bleed onto the fabric or canvas if not dry). Then join the desired number of plies before stitching.

STITCHING INFORMATION

Stab Stitch/Sewing Stitch

If you chose to use a hoop or frame, you will need to use the stab stitch method to stitch your project. This simply means you place one stitch at a time. You bring the needle up from the wrong side and go down into the fabric or canvas from the right side to work the stitch.

If not using a hoop, you can use the sewing method. Simply slide the needle in and out of the fabric using shallow stitches.

Thread Tension

Thread tension is a concern for every stitcher. Try to keep the tension consistent on all your stitches. Hold your fabric or canvas so you have a side view (front and back) of the stitches. Are any stitches of the same type, and with the same thread, higher or lower than the rest? If they are uneven, the tension is not consistent. Do your stitches appear the same? Do they appear to be pulling the fabric so it is wrinkling around the stitches or the canvas threads so they buckle? Does the stitching surface still lie flat? Are the stitches too loose? If you can run your needle under the thread and pull the stitch away from the fabric or canvas, it is too loose and you will need to pull your stitches a little tighter. Are the stitches too tight? Is it difficult to run your thread under your stitches on the back when ending your thread? This would indicate the tension is too tight. If this happens, loosen your tension just a little. Your stitches should be somewhere between too tight and too loose. Perfect tension requires patience and practice. One thing that helps is to learn to look at your needlework on the front and on the back every few stitches. If you make this a habit, you will be able to recognize when you are pulling the thread too tightly or leaving it too loose. The tension of a stitch is important in the finished piece. You can be an advanced stitcher or a beginning stitcher and not have a quality piece if the tension isn't correct.

Stab stitch

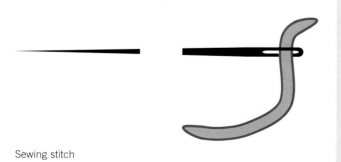

Sewing stitch

TENSION

If you find you are a stitcher who consistently pulls the stitches too tightly, always use a hoop or frame when stitching. Having a consistent tension and being sure your threads lie flat and are not twisted will help ensure a beautiful piece of needlework.

Laying the Thread

Although it is optional when stitching, laying thread with a laying tool creates a smoother look. Using a laying tool can be as simple as guiding the thread with your finger as it goes down into the fabric or canvas. You can also use a darning needle, stiletto, or a laying tool sold in needlework shops. Keeping the thread straight and smooth gives the stitch a nicer appearance. Stranded threads should lie next to each other without twisting over themselves.

To lay threads, bring the thread to the front side of the work. Place the laying tool under the thread. Take the thread to where it goes down into the fabric or canvas. Use the tool to gently work the thread in one direction as it goes into the hole of the canvas or the even-weave fabric. In order for the thread lie correctly, it must be smooth as it goes down into fabric or canvas and comes up out of the fabric or canvas.

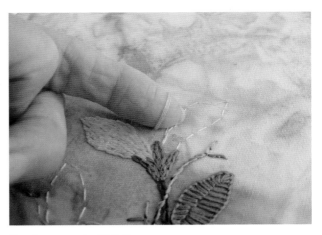

Your finger as a laying tool

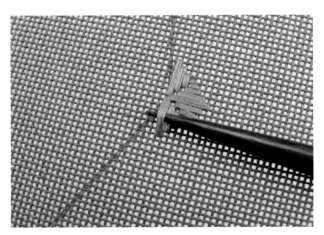

Using a laying tool

Beginning and Ending Threads

SMALL KNOT

Creative embroidery and crewel can all be started using a small knot.

Thread the needle and bring the tip end of the thread length up along the side of the needle so the end of the thread is toward your body and the point of the needle is straight up in the air. Hold the thread firmly next to the needle between your thumb and forefinger with your stitching hand grasping the middle of the needle. With the other hand, wrap the loose thread at the tip of your thumb around the end of the needle two or three times. (The number of wraps determines the size of the knot). Catch the end of the wrapped thread between your thumb and needle, and adjust the loose length of thread so it hangs downward along the needle. Hold the thread gently but firmly and pull the needle straight up with your stitching hand. The wrapped thread will slide down along the length of thread to form a small even knot at the tip end. Clip the tail of the thread near the knot. Hold the knot between your thumb and forefinger, and pull on the knot to be sure it is secure.

EASY KNOT

Thread the needle. Moisten the end of your index finger. Wrap the end of the thread around the index finger. Roll the thread between your index finger and thumb until twisted together, and slide the loop to the tip of your index finger. Grip the top of the loop between your index finger and thumb, and pull it down to the end of the thread to form the knot.

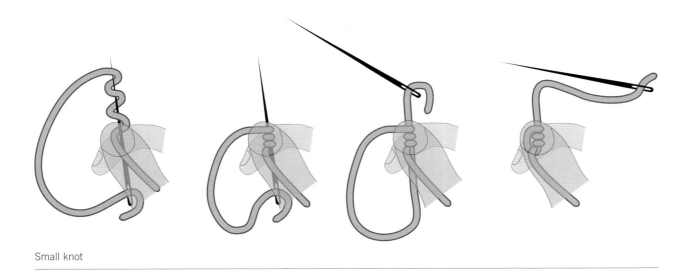

Small knot

WASTE KNOT

This type of knot can be used for any technique that uses plain- or even-weave fabric. Use a waste knot in areas where your stitches will cover the fabric. Put the needle down through the front side of your fabric in the area you will travel over. The knot should be 1" to 1½" (2.5 to 3.8 cm) away from the starting point. Bring the needle up from the back at your starting point and begin stitching, working over the thread toward the knot. When you reach the knot, clip it off and continue stitching.

Once the knot is clipped, it may be necessary, on the back, to clip the thread closer to the last stitch placed. This will keep the fuzzy end of the thread from pulling to the front with the next stitch placed.

AWAY WASTE KNOT

Cross-stitch can be started with an away waste knot.

Tie a knot in the end of your thread and move 2" or 3" (5.1 or 7.6 cm) away from the stitching area. Put the needle down through the front of the fabric. Come up from the back of the fabric with your needle at the starting point and begin stitching. When you have finished stitching, clip the waste knot on the front of the fabric, and weave the thread under the stitching on the back to secure. This knot is the same as a waste knot, only it is placed further away from the working area.

Once you have an area stitched, this method can be used for any of the techniques. Simply weave the new thread length into the previously stitched work for about an inch (2.5 cm) to secure. Then begin stitching, being careful for the first couple of stitches so you don't pull the thread tail out. If this project is one that will be washed many times, use a different method to begin so the thread is more secure.

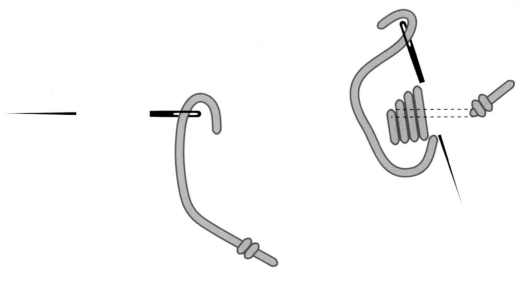

Waste knot

WEAVING UNDER TO END

Use this method to end thread for crewel, creative embroidery, and cross-stitch. If the project isn't going to be washed or have heavy use, you can simply weave the thread under several previously placed stitches on the back of the fabric. If the project is going to be washed, use a loop knot before clipping the thread.

ENDING SLIPPERY THREADS

To secure metallic, metallic braids, satin, and cotton pearl thread, run the thread under several stitches on the back of the fabric or canvas, and then take two backstitches over the thread of previously worked stitches. Be careful not to disrupt the stitches on the front.

LOOP KNOT

For a more secure ending, use a loop knot to end the thread. On the back of the fabric, weave the thread under several previously placed stitches. Then take the needle and thread around the stitch, slipping the needle through the looped end of the thread. Pull thread to secure the knot.

Removing Stitches

All stitchers at some point decide to rip out thread. This is simply part of the life of a stitcher. You may decide you do not like a type or color of thread. Or you feel you can do nicer stitching on the project. Whatever your reason, when you rip, use a blunt needle to help pull the stitch out of the fabric. As you pull the stitches out, clip the thread to shorten it if it is long; this will make it easier to pull out. It is never a good idea to use scissors to cut out thread, as you run the risk of cutting the fabric in addition to the thread. Use a new piece of thread to stitch the ripped area.

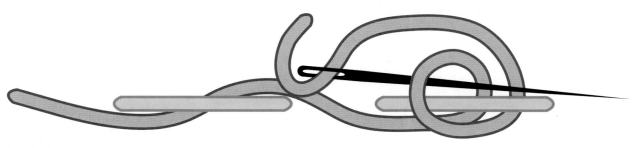

Loop knot

CREATIVE EMBROIDERY

Creative embroidery is a free form of embroidery that does not require counting. It is both easy to learn and fun to stitch. The stitches have soft appeal, as they flow freely across the fabric. If this is your first venture into needlework, this form of embroidery is an excellent place to start. The stitches in this chapter are easy to learn and the projects work up quickly.

Creative embroidery can be worked on any surface that a needle can slide through. Plain-weave fabric with a higher thread count gives a nice crisp finish to a project. All types of premade items can be embellished with embroidery, from kitchen towels to clothing to fabric shoes.

stitches

For the best results, work each stitch following the stitch graph numbers and arrows. When stitching, remember that the fabric should lie flat without pulling or wrinkling around the stitches. Refer to the information on tension (page 39).

Embroidery, crewel, and small chenille needles can be used for this technique. A tapestry needle works well to add the whipped or laced part of a stitch. If embellishing with beads, use a size 10 milliner or a short beading needle. For more information on needles, refer to page 10.

Stitches shown in creative embroidery and crewel are interchangeable. All the stitches in this chapter can be worked on even-weave fabric.

STRAIGHT

Straight stitches can be used to create motifs and darning patterns and can be worked in any direction. Bring the needle out at the starting point and take the needle and thread across the fabric for the desired stitch length of less than ¾" (1.9 cm). A longer stitch will give the appearance of an untidy loose stitch. This stitch does not conform to curved lines; avoid using it with even a short curved line, as you will lose the curve with a straight stitch.

You can use any type of thread for this stitch.

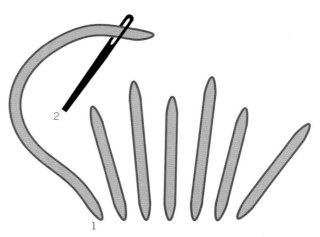

Ways to use: grass, leaves for small flowers, insect antennae, geometric patterns

Also known as: stroke stitch or single satin stitch

STEM

Travel from left to right, covering the pattern line. It is important to keep the thread below the needle, sewing the stitch by sliding the needle in and out of the fabric. The stitches are placed very close together to create the stem effect.

When working a curved line, place the stitches directly on the basted or drawn line. When using stranded thread, be sure that all the threads of each individual stitch are pulled using the same tension to maintain a smooth stitch. Pearl cotton will give this stitch a textured appearance.

Vary the stitch length in different areas of a design. Small stitches will give a more delicate look while longer, larger stitches give a bolder look. Example: Use a long stitch for tree trunks, large branches, or house roofs. You can use any type of thread for this stitch.

Ways to use: branches, flower stems, outlines, filling (leaves, flowers), lettering

Also known as: crewel, stalk

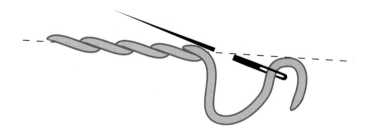

Keeping stitches close together

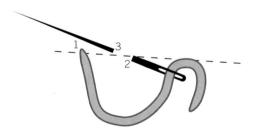

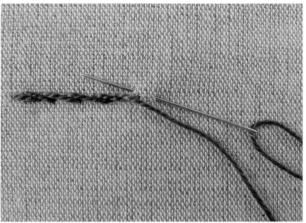

SPLIT

This is a versatile stitch that travels left to right. How you place the split in the stitch will determine how the stitch looks. You can work the stitch so the split comes in the center area, or the split can be placed closer to the end of the stitch. When working curved areas, a smaller stitch should be used. When working around a curve, take care to place the split in the center area of the stitch between the strands of threads.

The split is used as a filling stitch. It can be gradually shaded, or bands of one color in distinct shades can be used to create an attractive effect. For filling in areas, branches, or stems, split the stitch closer to the end of the stitch to give it a smoother look.

To achieve a smooth, even look in each stitch, use strands of a soft twisted thread or stranded thread. Use at least three strands of embroidery floss.

Ways to use: curved lines, straight lines, outlines, filling (closely worked rows) of flower petals, leaves, stems, branches, various shapes

Also known as: Kensington outline

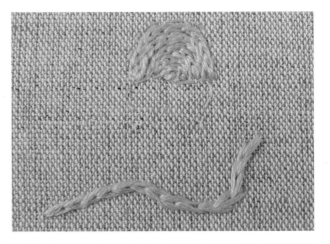

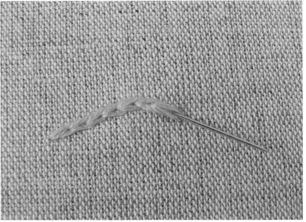

Needle comes up through previous stitch

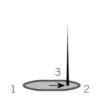
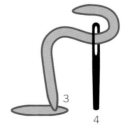

SATIN

Work this stitch diagonally, vertically, or horizontally, traveling left to right. It should be worked in small areas. If you would like to work a larger area, break it up into smaller sections. Place the stitches close together, keeping them flat as you work the area. When the stitching is completed, the threads should lie side by side, flat against each other. Hold the work at a slant to see if the threads are smooth and even across the top of the area.

Although the satin stitch looks like one of the simplest stitches, it is actually one of the most difficult stitches to work correctly. The challenge lies in keeping the tension correct and the stitches neat along the edges. The tension needs to be spot-on, which is very difficult to maintain while working a border area or filling in a leaf or flower petal. While some stitchers do find this stitch easy to work, many are put to the test with this stitch. It's worth the effort to master because, when worked correctly, the satin stitch is one of the most beautiful stitches.

An alternative method for the satin is to work a split stitch around the area and then thread the stitch through these stitches, as shown in the Crewel chapter (page 79). This method was originally used for shadow work but has become popular to use for other techniques.

You can use any type of thread for this stitch. Silk and pearl cotton (smaller size) threads give the stitch a lovely glow.

Ways to use: monogrammed initials, small borders, especially filling flower petals and leaves

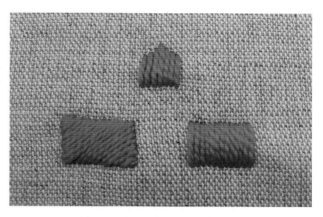

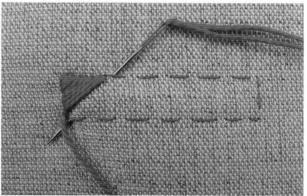

Filling in a shape

TAKE A BREAK

If you are having trouble with a stitch, put the work down and take a break. When you return, you'll likely find that it's much easier.

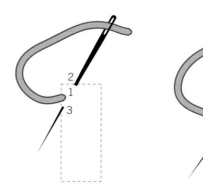

TWISTED SATIN

This is a beautiful stitch that is easy and fun to work. Work this stitch diagonally, horizontally, or circularly, traveling left to right. Twisting the satin stitch gives a textured look to the stitch.

Be careful not to pull the straight stitch too snug. For the twisted stitch, keep it slightly loose so the twist in the thread is visible.

Twisted threads work well for this stitch, but any type of thread can be used.

Ways to use: borders, motifs, filling, flowers, leaves

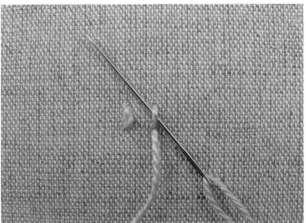
Threading the twist

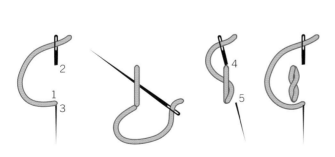

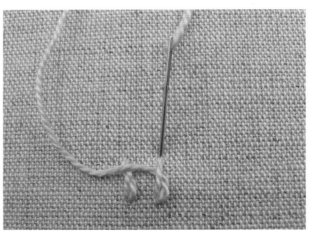
Ending the stitch

RUNNING

This simple stitch is worked by sliding the needle in and out of the fabric in a sewing motion. Travel right to left across the area. If using an even-weave fabric, each stitch should be the same length and spaced evenly along the line stitched. If using plain-weave fabric, make the stitch on the top side of the fabric longer than the stitch on the back, keeping the stitch length as even as possible. The length of the stitch will depend on the texture of the fabric and the thread being used. For straight-line stitch work, use a stitch length that is ¼" (6 mm) or less. If it is an outline stitch, it should be a small stitch to conform to the line being covered and stitches should fit evenly along the line, as in the swirl shown here. You can use any type of thread for this stitch.

Ways to use: outlining, borders, foundation for other stitches, bands, straight lines, curved lines

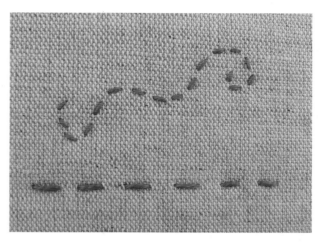

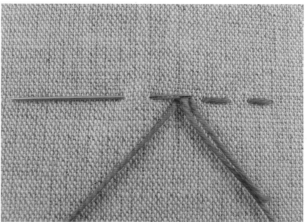

Keeping the stitches straight

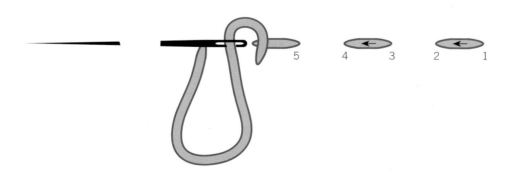

LONG AND SHORT

This is a variation of a satin stitch with the stitches worked in an uneven pattern. Travel left to right. For the first row of stitches, alternate a short and long stitch across the top of the area to be filled in. For the remaining rows, work long stitches. The example shown is the traditional long and short stitch. To create the traditional look, keep the short stitches the same length; and work all the long stitches the same length throughout the area. For the long and short stitch to be effective, there needs to be a distinct difference between the two sizes of stitches.

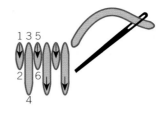

After the first row is in place, work down the shape to be filled in. Place the outside stitches first; then fill in the area between these stitches. Work small sections of the area this way as you work down the shape.

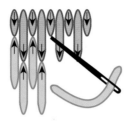
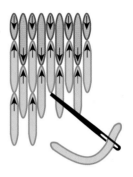

For working uneven shapes (flower petals with curves), adjust the size of your stitches to fit the shape. Place some shorter and some longer stitches when working down a flower petal, especially if the petal is long and narrow. You can also vary the length of the stitches to give more texture to the area when using embroidery floss. If worked this way, you will not have the set pattern look of the long and short stitch.

Shading the area is what gives this stitch its beauty. Shade the chosen color light to dark and divide the shape into two or three sections. The traditional way is three sections with three shades. If working more than one flower in a design, use only two colors for one of the flowers, giving that flower a slightly different look.

You can use any type of thread for this stitch. Pearl cotton and embroidery floss work well.

Ways to use: filling

Also known as: embroidery stitch, shading stitch, plumage stitch

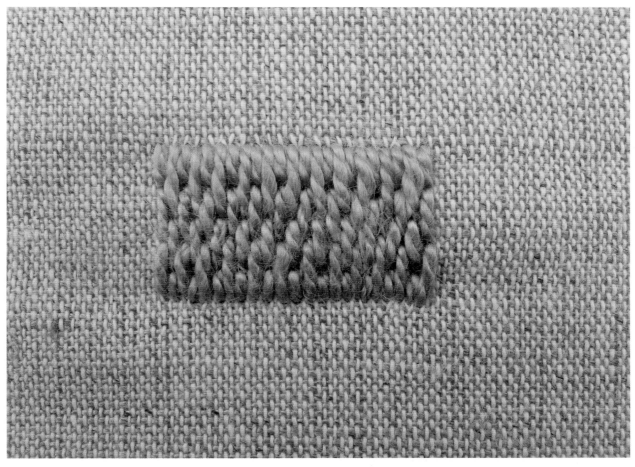

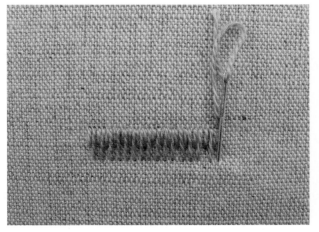

Alternating long and short stitches

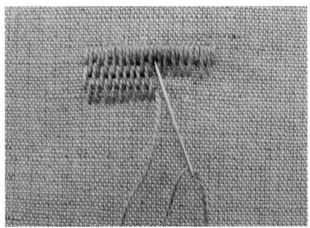

Placing long stitches

BACKSTITCH

Although the individual stitch goes to the left, the travel path goes from left to right—hence the name backstitch. Begin stitching a stitch length from the starting point. Work the first stitch back over to the starting point and down into the fabric. Each additional stitch is started a stitch length away from the previous stitch. When the area is completed, all stitches are snug against each other. The stitches should resemble a machine-sewn stitch.

This is a very versatile stitch and can be used in decorative ways. It is easiest worked on an even-weave fabric. It is a stunning stitch when worked on plain-weave. Do keep the stitches on plain-weave as straight and neat as possible, with each stitch the same length. It is best not to use a nubby or fuzzy thread. Twisted threads give the most textured look to the stitch. You can use any type of thread for this stitch.

Ways to use: outline (shown), stems, filling in branches (to add texture), details within motifs, flower petals

Also known as: Point De Sable, stitching, darning pattern

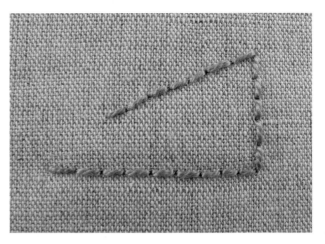

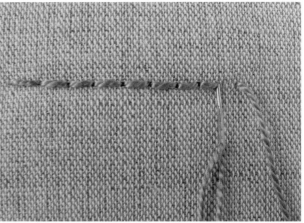

Traveling left to right

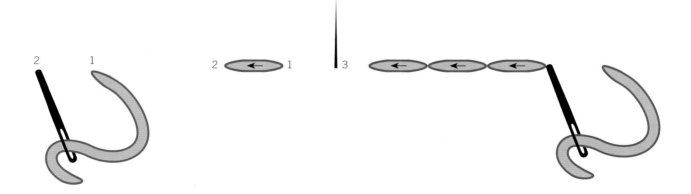

ZIGZAG BACKSTITCH

This stitch travels left to right. Although it is worked in a slightly different way, it has the rhythm of the backstitch. Stitch length can vary according to the fabric or canvas used. Follow the numbers when working the stitch to keep the back threads from showing through on sheer fabrics or open weaves. When using this stitch for a band, use a ¼" (6 mm) stitch length.

For a border stitch, as shown, turn the fabric upside down after working the first row. Work a second row, placing the bottom tip of the stitches of this row of zigzags snug to the first row to create a diamond. Do not split the thread of the previously placed stitches as you work. After the diamond effect is created, you can add a French knot (page 68) in the center and a row of the split stitch (page 48) ¼" (6 mm) or so from the top and bottom of the diamonds so it becomes a lovely border stitch. You can use any type of thread for this stitch.

Ways to use: bands, borders, background filling

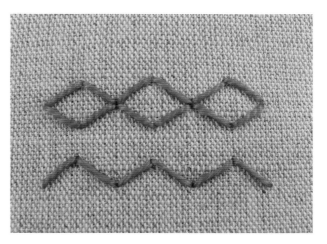

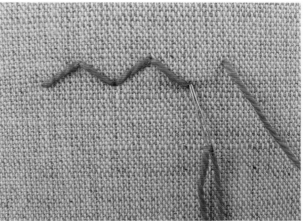

Sharing hole with previous stitch

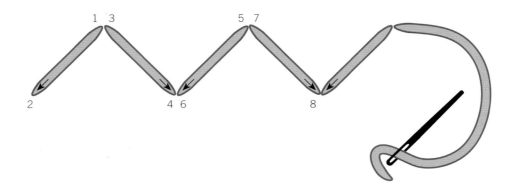

BLANKET

This stitch travels left to right. When working on a plain-weave fabric, keep the vertical stitches straight and the same height, and place the horizontal stitches the same distance apart. Keep the bottom loop of the thread pulled at the same tension. The stitch height is determined by how the stitch is used. Decorative stitches can be slightly longer or shorter, as shown. If using the stitch to close two pieces of fabric or felt to create a pillow, a smaller stitch length will be necessary.

Set your imagination loose when working this stitch. Use different heights to form a peak or rounded look to the stitch. Or simply place three short stitches together before repeating the pattern. On a piece of paper draw variations of the stitch. It's fun to play around with this stitch.

You can use any type of thread for this stitch. Pearl cotton and single-strand threads work best.

Ways to use: edgings, filling for flowers and leaves, bands, outlines

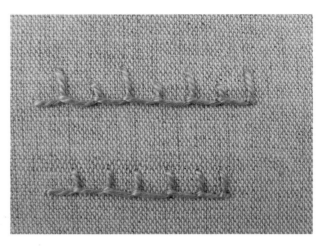

Keeping thread under needle

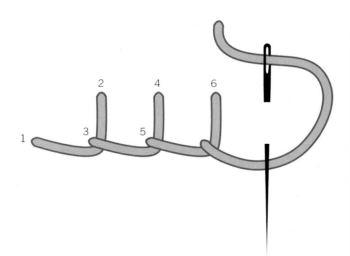

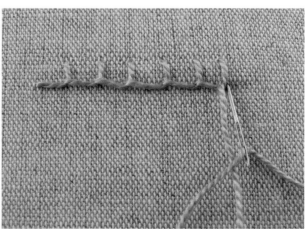

Ending the row

CLOSED BLANKET

This stitch, which travels left to right, is worked similarly to the blanket stitch. The vertical stitches of each set of stitches share a hole without piercing the thread of the first stitch placed. The right stitch is placed at a slight angle to connect over to the first vertical stitch in each stitch. As you work the stitch, always keep the thread under the needle on the downward stitch. Keep the stitches the same distance apart as you work across the area.

You can use any type of thread for this stitch.

Pearl cotton and single-strand threads work well for this stitch.

Ways to use: decorative hems, borders, bands, edgings

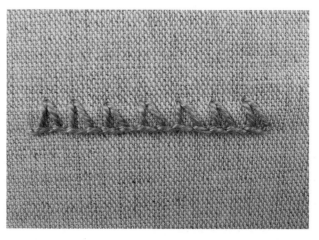

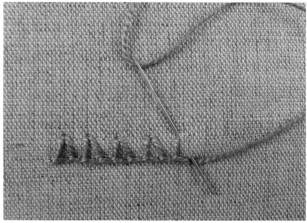

Slant the needle to create the closed stitch

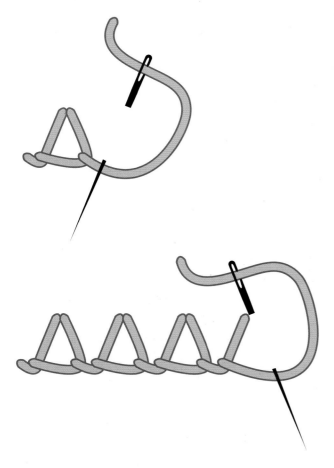

COUCHING

This stitch travels left to right around the area to be couched. A couching stitch is a straight stitch placed over the laid thread or threads to be secured to the fabric. If possible when working the couching stitch, come up and go down in the same hole or area under the laid thread.

Metallic braids add a touch of sparkle to the couching. If the couching thread is not used for a decorative purpose but to simply hold the thread or braid in place, use the same color of thread or braid for the couching stitches.

To create a fancy couching effect for decorative braids, use a cross-stitch (page 83), zigzag back (page 55), or lazy daisy (page 63) to hold the braid in place.

Pearl cotton and single-strand threads work best.

Ways to use: decorative swirls, filling shapes, secure lacing threads and decorative braids

Also known as: basic couching, plain couching

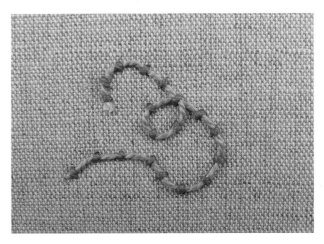

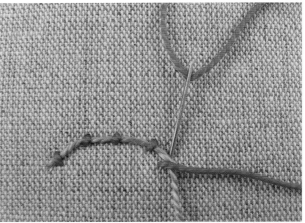

Couching over laid thread

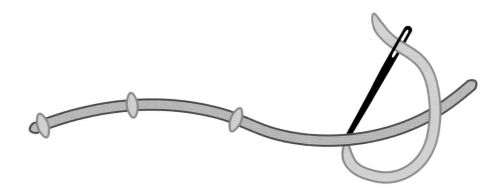

FERN

This is a fun stitch to use! You can travel in any direction, working the stitch from top to bottom. The straight stitches can be worked as a single unit or in a length of stitches. If you find the sewing method uncomfortable to find the rhythm of the stitch, use the stab method. The length of the stitches can be worked evenly or as required for the area. When working around a tight curve, as shown, the side diagonal stitches should be worked at slightly less of an angle. In some places, the center straight stitch will need to be slightly shorter to fit within the area.

You can use any type of thread for this stitch.

Ways to use: borders, filling, foliage, motifs, scrolling background patterns, veins of leaves

Working side stitch

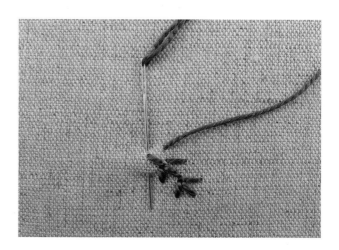

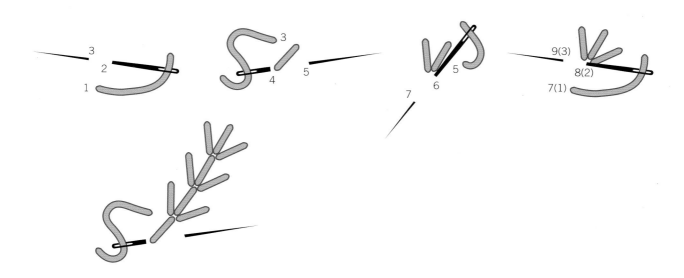

LEAF

Work this stitch from the bottom upward. If working a band or border, travel left to right. This stitch conforms to the shape it is filling and has a slight slant to the straight stitches.

This is a beautiful flat leaf stitch to use when you would like to have a leaf that appears translucent. When working this stitch, it is important to leave space enough between the stitches. Each stitch has a slant and the stitches cross over each other in the center. The hardest part of working this stitch is being careful to crisscross the thread over far enough in the center area. For best results, practice this stitch on a scrap of fabric to learn the rhythm of the stitch in the center area.

To use as a border stitch on plain fabric, you may want to baste three lines parallel to each other and spaced an equal distance apart. Work the stitches between the lines in the same manner as shown for the leaf.

You can use any type of thread for this stitch. Pearl cotton or hand-dyed single-strand threads give a smooth look to the stitch.

Ways to use: filling, leaf shapes, borders

Also known as: fir

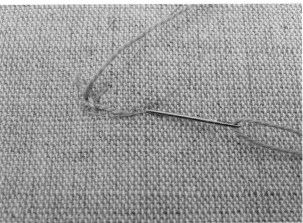

Starting leaf

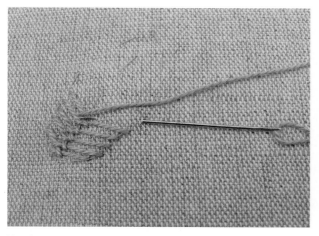

Keeping crossover consistent

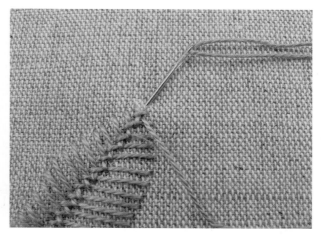

Ending leaf

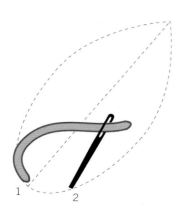

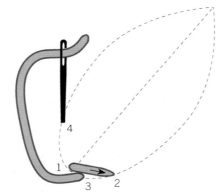

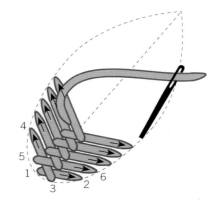

FEATHER

There are many feather stitches with this stitch as their foundation. Travel in a vertical, horizontal, circular, or curved direction, working top to bottom. It is important to keep both sides even in height. Keep the stitch size the same or vary the size, depending on the desired look. The rhythm of this stitch works well with the sewing method as you place the stitches on alternate sides. Use your finger to hold the thread in place while completing the stitch.

You can use any type of thread for this stitch.

Ways to use: light filling, borders, outlines, circular motifs, grass, ferns, leaves, embellishment on clothing, as an appliqué stitch, bird feathers

Also known as: single coral, briar, plumage

Working curved shape

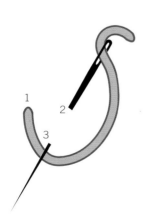 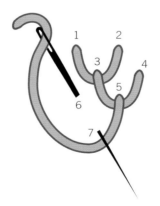 

LAZY DAISY

This stitch can be worked in any direction. It is worked like a chain stitch and is anchored with a small vertical tie-down stitch. For a neater stitch, keep the ends of the loop together where they meet at the top. When working a flower petal, use the same hole for the two ends of the loop. How you work this stitch will depend on the look you want to achieve. You'll need to use your finger to hold the left side of the loop in place while you complete the stitch. Add a straight stitch in the middle of the loop for a filled lazy daisy.

This versatile stitch can be used alone or grouped together.

You can use any type of thread for this stitch.

Ways to use: filling, flower petals, buds, leaves, bands

Also known as: detached chain, tail chain, knotted knot, daisy, loop, picot, tied loop

Working loop

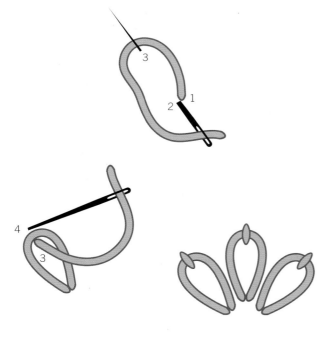

Filling in loop

CHAIN

Travel in any direction, working top to bottom. Keep the ends of the loop even or share the same hole. It is worked similarly to the lazy daisy. If you are working the stitch correctly, only back-stitches should be visible on the back. Use your finger to hold the thread in place while completing the stitch. The stitch should lie flat against the fabric, and the fabric should not pucker.

When using this stitch as a filling stitch for flowers or leaves, start each row at the tip of the leaf or petal, working all the rows in this manner. For border stitches, work different size chains together. Work a short stitch, a long stitch, and repeat the pattern. This variation is shown. You can also vary the stitch by working a long stitch and two short stitches; then repeat. You can use any type of thread for this stitch.

Ways to use: borders, curved motifs, circular shapes, filling, outlines

Also known as: tambour, point de chainette

Working chain

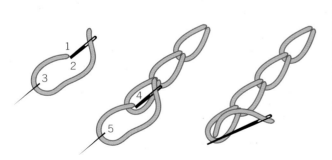

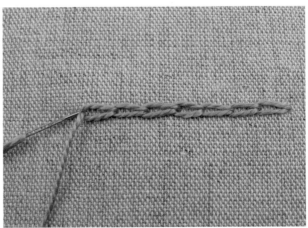

Ending chain

BACKSTITCHED CHAIN

Travel in any direction, working top to bottom. Keep the ends of the loop even or share the same hole. Work the chain stitch first; then place the backstitches. Use your finger to hold the thread in place while completing the stitch. The backstitches inside the chain can be worked with small stitches, as shown, or with stitches that touch each other and fill the area. This stitch is most effective if two colors and two textures of thread are used.

You can use any type of thread for the chain stitch. Metallic braid and pearl cotton work especially well for backstitches.

Ways to use: bands, outlines, clothing

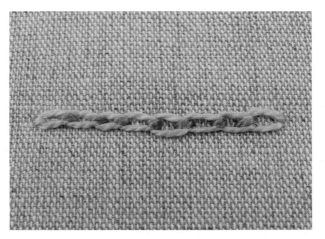

Working chain

Working backstitch

SPINE

This is a quick and easy decorative version of the chain stitch. Travel in any direction, working top to bottom.

Keep the stitch flat against the fabric. When you work the angled spine, work it slightly above the bottom of the chain stitch. The next chain stitch will be placed below the straight spine stitch.

The straight spine part of the stitch can be worked on every other chain stitch, as shown, or worked all on one side or both sides.

You can use any type of thread for this stitch.

Ways to use: borders, outline, filling

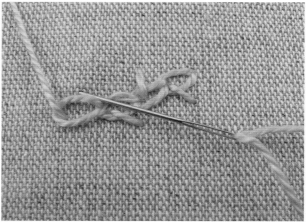

Working straight spine

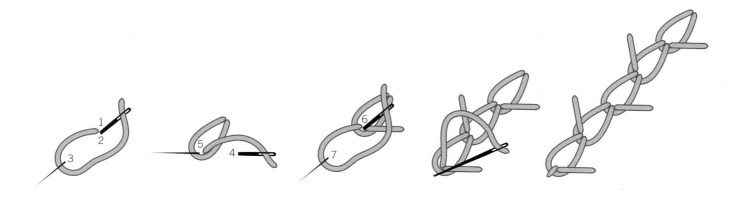

PISTIL

This is an easy stitch to work and can be worked in any direction. It is a variation of a French knot with an added stem. This stitch is usually used in crewel work but it is too pretty to be limited to that technique.

When working this stitch, you can use any length of stem that works for the application. When using on a curved line, as you take the needle down into the fabric have the thread for the stem slightly loose to conform to the area. For a straight pistil, keep the stem thread and wrapped thread taut as it enters the fabric.

You can use any type of thread for this stitch. Twisted threads give a crisp look to the stitch.

Ways to use: flower stamens, flower petals, fillers

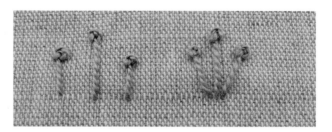

Starting needle into fabric

Keeping thread taunt

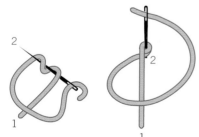

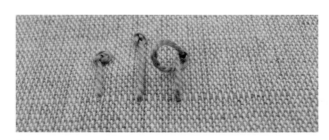

Pulling thread into fabric

FRENCH KNOT

Place knot where desired. The size of thread and number of wraps will determine the knot size produced. Use one, two, or three wraps depending on your desired knot size. Once the thread is wrapped on the needle, it is important to keep the needle straight and the thread taut as it enters the fabric. Use your other hand to hold the thread taut. Practice this stitch on a scrap of fabric using a thick thread. When you master the knot this way, you can use any type of thread in your projects. For best results, work this stitch in a hoop or frame.

To create a sloppy knot, leave the wrapped thread loose as you pull it down into the fabric. You can change the size of the knot by adjusting the tension used when wrapping. It is used for flower buds, centers of larger flowers, and to fill in areas. You can mix the two types of knots when filling areas to add texture. The lower right knot in the group of three is a sloppy knot.

You can use any type of thread for this stitch. French knots made with rayon or other synthetic threads are beautiful. Although this slippery thread is a little more difficult to use, the results are well worth the effort!

Ways to use: flower centers, filling, single row of knots spaced for outline of leaves or shapes

Also known as: French dot, knotted, twisted knot, wound

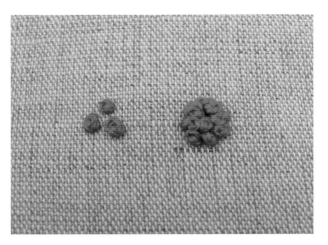

Starting needle into fabric

Keeping thread taunt

Pulling thread into fabric

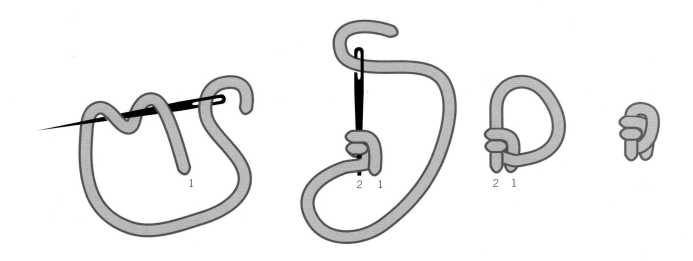

EMBROIDERED JACKET COLLAR

This simple design adds color to the deep indigo blue of the jacket. The embroidery embellishment gives the jacket a touch of elegance, making it perfect for a day at the office or an evening out. This pattern can be used as a border for pillowcases, on a small pillow, or on any garment. Increase the pattern for larger areas.

YOU WILL NEED

- jacket, blouse, or vest
- hand-dyed single-strand cotton: guacamole
- six-strand embroidery floss: avocado green, very light topaz, medium electric blue
- embroidery or crewel needle

STITCHES USED

- chain
- French knot
- lazy daisy
- stem
- straight

STITCHING INFORMATION

1 Transfer the design, using the tissue tracing method (page 37). Center and baste the pattern through the tissue paper onto the label of the jacket.

2 Use one strand of the guacamole single-strand cotton and the stem stitch to work the flower stem.

3 Use three strands of the avocado green embroidery floss and the straight stitch to work the flower leaves on the stem.

4 Use two strands of the blue embroidery floss and the chain stitch to work the four-petal flowers.

5 Use one strand of the topaz embroidery floss and the French knot to work the three knots in the center of each flower. Wrap the thread around the needle three times instead of the usual two times.

6 Use four strands of the blue embroidery floss and the lazy daisy to work the bud flowers.

Design pattern (actual size)

EXTRA TOUCH

For added embellishment on the jacket, embroider a section of the pattern on the opposite side on the collar, above the lapel area. Or, work one bud, stem, and leaf under the pocket opening.

EMBELLISHED PILLOW CASE

Sunshine yellow brings a blaze of color to any room with this cheerful design. Customize the flower colors to fit your décor. You can increase or decrease the pattern size to fit your pillow. A purchased pillow that includes a pillow sham makes finishing a snap.

YOU WILL NEED

- 17½" × 13½" (44.5 × 34.3 cm) premade pillow with a sham cover
- 13" × 13" (33.0 × 33.0 cm) light blue batik fabric (adjust the fabric size if using hoop or frame), finished size 9" × 7" (22.9 × 17.8 cm)
- non-fusible stabilizer cut to size of fabric
- six-strand embroidery floss: lemon, light lemon, light avocado green, topaz, royal blue, very dark parrot green, medium parrot green, and bright canary
- stranded satin: ultralight avocado green
- pearl cotton, size 8: medium delft blue
- embroidery or crewel needle

STITCHES USED

- blanket
- chain
- French knot
- lazy daisy
- long and short
- pistil
- stem

Design pattern (actual size)

STITCHING INFORMATION

1 Transfer the design using non-fusible transfer method (page 37). Do not trace the small dots or stamens on the pattern. These will be worked freehand.

2 Use three strands of the very dark parrot green embroidery floss and the chain stitch to work the flower stem, stopping at the five-petal flower and two sepals.

3 Use three strands of the medium parrot green embroidery floss and the chain stitch to work the two sepals.

4 Use two strands of the avocado green stranded satin and the stem stitch to work the stem and the short branches of the vine that wrap around the flower stem. Place two straight stitches at the tip of each branch.

5 Use three strands of the medium parrot green embroidery floss and the blanket stitch to work the leaves on the flower stem. Start the blanket stitch at the tip of the leaf and work the straight horizontal part of the stitch over to the center vein. Keep stitches close together to cover the material. (A)

B

6 Use three strands of embroidery floss for the flowers and two strands for the bud. Work the long and short stitch shading as follows: Three-petal flower, use light lemon and lemon. Five-petal flower, use light lemon, lemon, and bright canary. Bud, use light lemon, lemon, and bright canary. Start with the lightest color at the flower tips and work toward the center of the flower. Refer to the photograph for shading on the flowers and bud.

7 Use two strands of the topaz embroidery floss and the pistil stitch to work the stamens on the flowers. (B)

8 Use two strands of the light avocado green embroidery floss and the French knot stitch to work the base of the flowers on the vine.

9 Use four strands of the royal blue embroidery floss and the lazy daisy stitch to work the vine flowers.

FINISHING

10 Trim fabric to 9" × 7" (22.9 × 17.8 cm), following the grainlines as closely as possible. Place in the center of sham, and pin in place. (C)

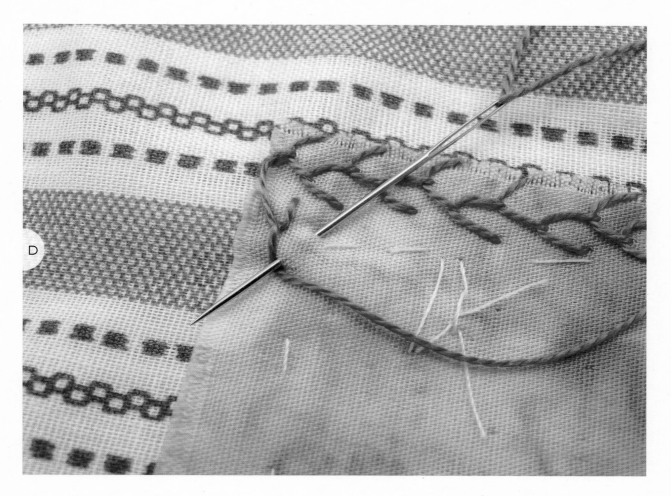

11 Leave the edges of the fabric raw; gently
remove any loose threads on fabric edges.
Use the blue pearl cotton and the feather stitch
to attach the fabric to the pillow. (D)

CREWEL

XXXXXXXXXXXXXXXXXXXXXXXXXXXXXXXX

Crewel is the sister of creative embroidery. The word "crewel" is derived from an old Welsh word meaning wool. Even in this century, crewel projects must include a wool thread, wool-blended threads, or wool yarn to be termed crewel. Keep in mind that projects containing wool need to be dry-cleaned.

The traditional crewel technique was and is worked with wool thread or Persian yarn on 100 percent linen twill. This very heavy fabric has a distinctive look with a diagonal pattern weave on both sides of the fabric. When using a bright or colorful fabric for crewel, use soft, lighter tones for the threads and yarn.

NO-NO

Regular knitting yarns will not work for stitching crewel or needlepoint. Such yarn is stretchy and does not allow you to maintain the correct tension. The friction of the stitching motion will break down the fiber before the area is completed.

stitches

This technique includes a few nontraditional stitches. The feather stitch is used mainly for creative embroidery. It adds charm to the crewel work and looks simply beautiful when stitched in wool and wool blends.

Chenille or crewel needles work well. When stitching with 100 percent wool, wool blends, or Persian yarn, use a needle with a larger eye. A tapestry needle works well when working the whipped, laced, threaded, and woven stitches.

STRAIGHT

This stitch can be worked in any direction, from top to bottom or bottom to top or even sideways. There is not a set way to work the stitch. A straight stitch does not conform to curved lines and should not be used for long stitches. When using yarn for small, short stitches, use a slightly loose tension so they do not become stubby.

You can use any type of thread for this stitch. Wool thread will give a smoother appearance to the stitch than a Persian yarn.

Ways to use: grass, leaves for small flowers, insect antennae, geometric patterns, anywhere a straight line is needed

Also known as: stroke stitch or single satin stitch

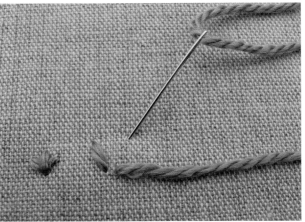

Completing stitch

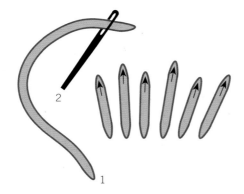

SEED

Work these small stitches randomly in different directions, without a given pattern. For best results, work small, straight even stitches. This stitch works up quickly, creating a light airy effect in the desired shape. If a shaded effect is desired, use light and dark tones of the same color.

You can use any type of thread for this stitch. Wool thread creates a small stitch, as shown above.

Ways to use: flower petals, leaves, background, shapes, monogram letters

Also known as: seed filling, speckling, rice grain, dot stitch

Seeding an area

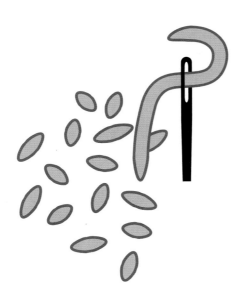

DOUBLE SEED

Work small side-by-side stitches randomly across the area. Place the double stitches so they go in various directions without a set pattern. Keep them close together and as even in length as possible.

You can use any type of thread for this stitch. Wool thread creates a small stitch, as shown above.

Ways to use: flower petals, leaves, background, shapes, monogram letters

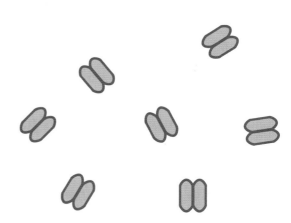

Keeping stitches parallel

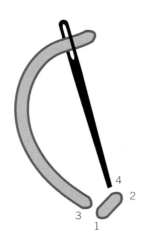

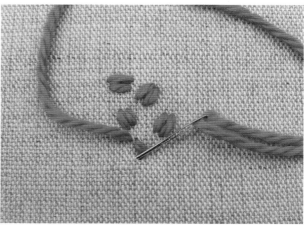

CROSS

This simple stitch can travel horizontally, vertically, or diagonally, or you can place single stitches randomly over the area. It is beautiful when used as a couching stitch, randomly placed for a filling stitch, or worked as a border stitch. It can be used in all techniques in this book. This stitch is normally used on an even-weave fabric for the cross-stitch technique (page 110). Try to work the stitches evenly. This is not easy to do on plain-weave fabric; the stitches may vary slightly on this fabric. Baste lines or use the quilter's tape marked with ¼" (6 mm) marks to keep the stitches even on plain-weave fabric.

Ways to use: borders, bands, filling

Also known as: sampler stitch

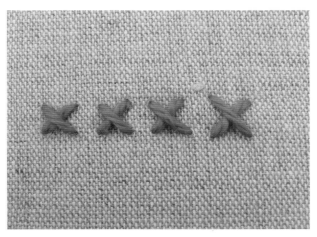

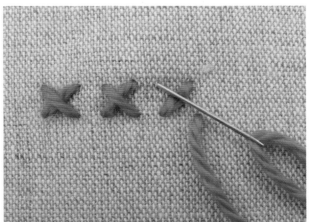

Completing the cross

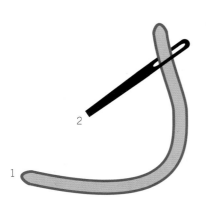

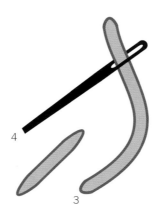

STEM

This is a very graceful stitch when worked in wool. Travel left to right across the line to be worked. When working curved lines or outlines, keep the stitch on the marked line. For all stem work, keep the thread below the needle at all times with the stitches close together.

You can use any thread for this stitch. For more texture, use pearl cotton, wool, or yarn.

Ways to use: branches, stems, outlines, filling, lettering

Also known as: crewel, stalk

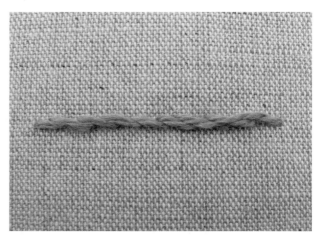

Creating a straight stem

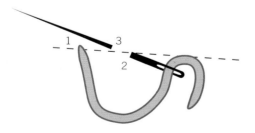

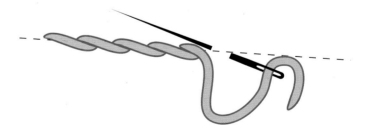

BLANKET PINWHEEL

This is a variation of the blanket stitch (see page 56 in Creative Embroidery) and it travels left to right. Draw a circle on tissue paper and then use this pattern to baste the outline in the area desired. Once the basting is in place and the paper removed, define the center of the circle. Work the needle back and forth between two stitches in the center to enlarge the opening. This will make stitching easier. Work the stitch in the same manner as the blanket stitch.

With thicker threads, as you work the vertical stitch to the center hole, it will be impossible to place them all in the center. Let every other one drop down slightly outside the circle. The next thread will cover it going down into the center hole.

You can use any type of thread for this stitch. Wool threads and pearl cotton work especially well.

Ways to use: flower centers, flowers (add stem), borders, circles

Also known as: wheel, blanket wheel, circle

Working around circle

BORDER WHEELS

For an eye-catching border stitch, work half circles of the blanket pinwheel. You can space them out or let the outer stitches touch.

KNOTTED BLANKET

This knotted variation of the blanket stitch travels left to right. It can be a little tricky to work, but it is worth learning. Keep the knot stitch secure on the needle while making the vertical stitch. The thread should be under the needle as you place the vertical stitch; at the same time pull the knot down into the fabric with the needle coming out and across the thread to make the horizontal part of the blanket stitch. The secret is to keep the thread taut around the needle. The height of the stitch can be worked even or varied. The stitches can be worked flat, in a circle, or on the edge of the fabric.

You can use any type of thread for this stitch. Wool threads work especially well.

Ways to use: filling, edging, bands, flower stamens, outlines

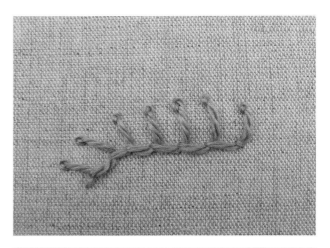

Working knot bringing needle out over horizontal thread

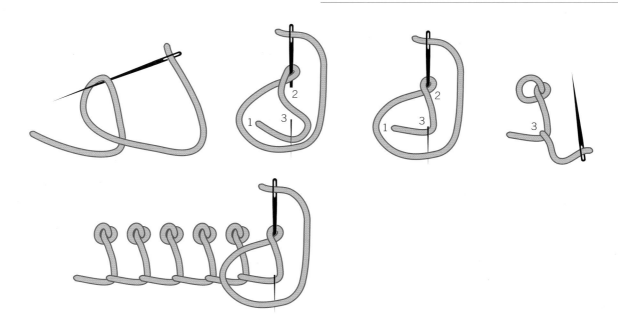

FEATHER

This stitch can travel in a vertical, horizontal, circular, or curved direction, working top to bottom. The most important step when working this stitch is to keep both ends of the stitch (at 1 and 2) even in height. Keep the stitch width the same or vary the size depending on the desired look. The rhythm of this stitch works well using the sewing method as you place the stitches on alternate sides. Use your finger to hold the thread in place while completing the stitch.

You can use any type of thread for this stitch. Wool thread and pearl cotton work especially well.

Ways to use: circular motifs, borders, outlines, light filling, grass, ferns, leaves, embellishment on clothing, as an appliqué stitch, bird feathers

Also known as: single coral, briar, plumage

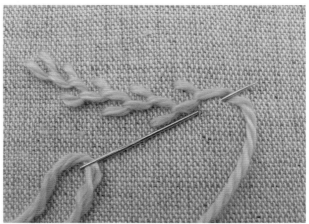

Working next stitch

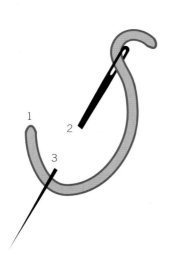

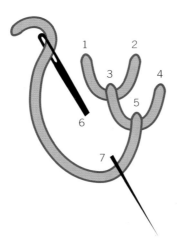

FISHBONE

This stitch travels top to bottom down the shape or bottom to top up the shape. The stitches should cross slightly to create a thickness in the center area. This stitch conforms well to any shape. It is a great stitch for small treetops. It should lie smooth against the fabric. It works well for borders worked horizontally across an area.

Fishbone works up quickly and works well with all types of thread. For some leaves, begin by putting a straight stitch at the tip. Then put the first fishbone stitch at a slight angle so it covers the tip. You can use any type of thread for this stitch. Pearl cotton and wool thread give texture to the stitch.

Ways to use: bones, small treetops, bands, borders, leaves

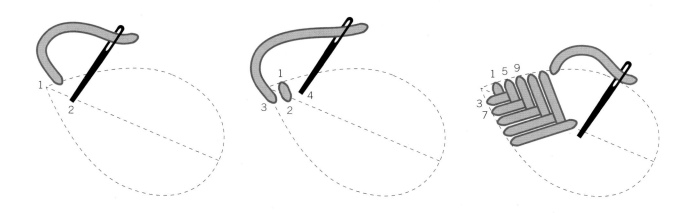

FANCY COUCHING

This stitch travels left to right around the area to be couched. You can use any decorative stitch that can be worked across a laid thread as a fancy couching stitch. Shown are three fancy couching stitches: the cross-stitch, angled, and zigzag stitches. These stitches can be placed at random distances or you can space them ¼" or ½" (6 mm or 1.3 cm) apart, or any distance you prefer.

Work the long laid thread first, securing it in place; then work the couching thread over the laid thread. As you work over the laid thread, place the couching stitch carefully and do not pull it too snug.

When couching over a larger area, use a longer thread and two needles. Use one needle for the laid thread, the other needle for the couching thread. Work small sections at a time.

You can use any type of thread for this stitch. Metallic braids add a touch of sparkle to the couching thread.

Ways to use: decorative swirls, filling shapes, secure lacing threads, and decorative braids

Also known as: basic couching, plain couching

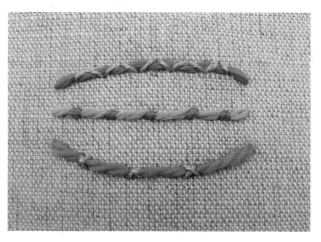

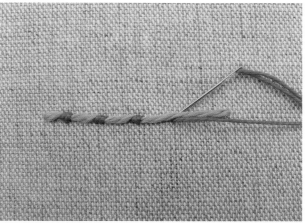

Angled stitch

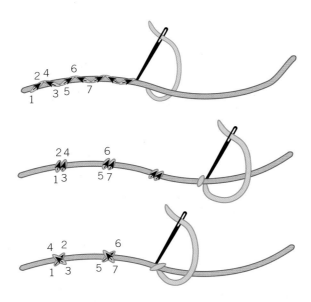

PETAL

This stitch is a combination of the daisy stitch and a straight or backstitch traveling right to left. It works well on straight or curved lines. Begin a stitch distance away from the starting point. Place the first stitch back toward that point. Come up halfway under the first stitch to make the daisy. Repeat this process across the area. End with the last daisy in the center or add an additional daisy at the tip of the last straight stitch for foliage.

Ways to use: stems, foliage, bands, circular or swirl motif, edging

Also known as: pendant chain

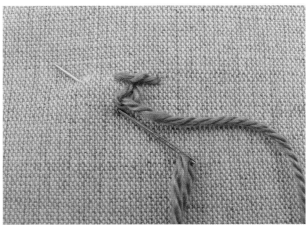

Completing first stitch

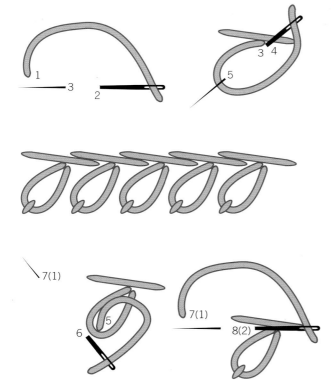

Starting second stitch

FRENCH KNOT

Place knot where desired. The size of thread and number of wraps will determine the knot size produced. Use one, two, or three wraps depending on your desired knot size. Once the thread is wrapped on the needle, it is important to keep the needle straight and the thread taut as it enters the fabric. Use your other hand to hold the thread taut. Practice this stitch on a scrap of fabric using a thick thread. When you master the knot this way, you can use any type of thread in your projects. For best results, work this stitch in a hoop or frame. You can use any type of thread for this stitch. Wool thread or Persian yarn is beautiful when used to fill leaves and flowers for crewel.

Ways to use: flower centers, filling, single row of knots spaced for outline of leaves or shapes

Also known as: French dot, knotted, twisted knot, wound

Starting into fabric

Keeping thread taut

Completing knot

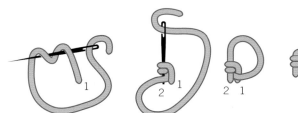

CORAL

This is the simplest of the knotted stitches and it travels right to left. Make the first knot very close to where you come up out of the fabric. Space the other knots at the same distance from each other across the area to be stitched. Do not pull the knot too snug or it will become distorted. When ending the stitch, place a long stitch at the end or end it next to the knot. The size of the vertical stitch (4–5) and the size of the thread determine the size of the knot.

You can use any type of thread for this stitch.

Ways to use: filling, outlines for motifs, leaves, flowers

Also known as: beaded knot, German knot, coral knot, snail trail, knotted outline

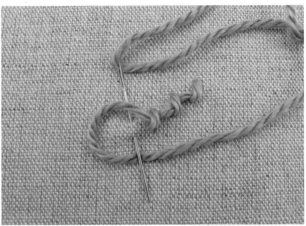

Forming knot

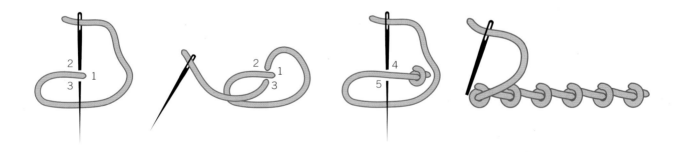

SWORD EDGING

These small stitches can be worked randomly in any direction or in a straight line or rows for a border stitch. When working the stitch, be sure the first stitch is long enough and slightly loose so it will pull down into place when the longer tail stitch slides over and then under it. When working in rows, offset the stitches of each row.

You can use any type of thread for this stitch.

Ways to use: filling, borders, bands

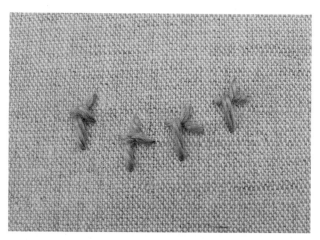

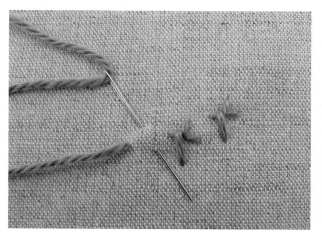

First stitch

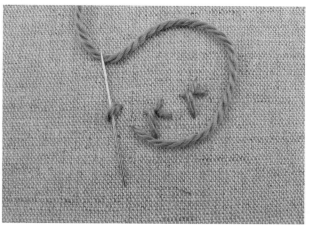

Threading under first stitch

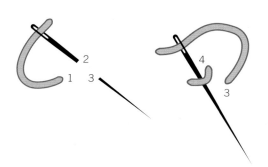
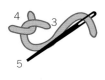

ROMANIAN

This stitch is worked horizontally and travels top to bottom. It conforms well to filling shapes and works up quickly. It is simply a straight stitch with a small tie-down stitch in the middle. Although the tie-down stitch should be in the center of the area, a little variance adds interest.

You can use any type of thread for this stitch. Wool or twisted threads work especially well.

Ways to use: borders, bands, filling (small shapes), leaves, flower petals

Also known as: Oriental, Romanian couching, antique, Janina, Indian filling

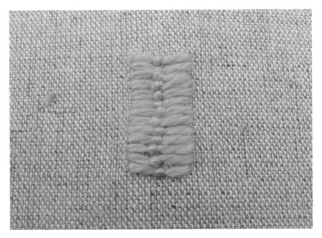

Extending a border

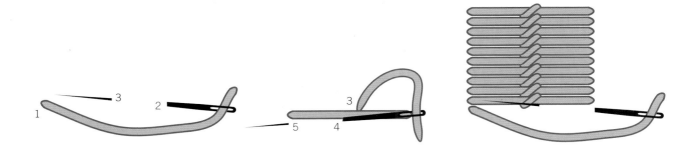

BOKHARA COUCHING

This versatile stitch can travel vertically or horizontally. It conforms well when filling shapes and works up quickly. It is worked the same as the Romanian stitch but is tied in several places. The number of tie-downs depends on the length of the base stitch.

Wool or wool blends, twisted or hand-dyed single-strand threads work best, but you can use any type of thread.

Ways to use: borders, bands, filling (small shapes), leaves, flower petals

Completing couch stitch and lining up for next stitch

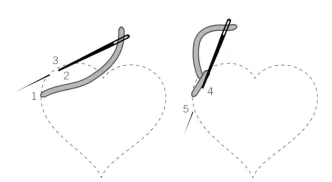

PAISLEYS AND PEARLS PILLOW

This project combines charcoal-polished cotton with wool threads and Swarovski pearls, creating an elegant pillow that will add color and excitement to any room. By simply changing the colors to go with the décor, this paisley design can fit with any color scheme! For an alternate color choice, use an antique white pillow with three shades of blue or raspberry. The paisley pattern can also be worked on any garment or home décor item. A variegated thread can be used to add interest.

YOU WILL NEED

- ✖ 18" × 12" (45.7 × 30.5 cm) premade pillow with a sham cover
- ✖ 100 percent wool thread: aqua, bright yellow, and orange red
- ✖ five pearls, size 6 mm: powdered almond
- ✖ sewing thread in aqua, red, and yellow
- ✖ Silamide bead thread, size A: medium gray
- ✖ crewel and beading needles

STITCHES USED

- ✖ stem
- ✖ feather
- ✖ seed

STITCHING INFORMATION

1 Remove the pillow insert. If not using a sham pillow, remove a few inches (cm) of stitches from the bottom seam and remove the stuffing from inside the pillow. Set insert or stuffing aside.

2 Transfer the pattern using the tissue tracing method (page 35). Trace three paisley patterns.

3 Lay the traced patterns on the pillow top and turn the paisleys, traced side down or up depending on the direction. Refer to photograph for placement. Pin the pattern in place and baste around the tissue paper.

4 Use yellow sewing thread to baste the smaller inside line of the pattern onto the fabric. Use the red sewing thread to baste the middle line, and aqua sewing thread to baste the outside line. When basting is complete, remove the tissue paper.

5 Use two strands of orange red wool and the stem stitch to stitch over the middle line of the paisley.

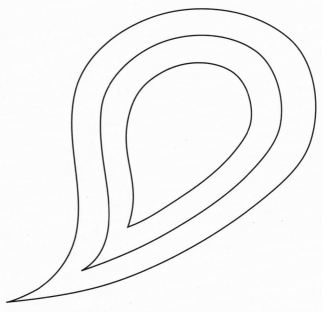

Paisley pattern (actual size)

ADJUSTABLE

Increase or decrease the pattern as needed to fit your project.

6 Use two strands of sunny yellow wool and the feather stitch to stitch over the yellow basted line. Begin stitching at the tip of the paisley point, placing a feather stitch on each side of the basted line. Work down one side to the halfway point, and secure the last feather stitch on this side by placing a small stitch over the loop end. Work down the other side until your stitches meet. When the two feather rows meet, they will be back to back with the loops close together. End the last feather stitch by taking a slightly longer stitch that goes over the small stitch of the opposite loop, joining the sides for a finished look. If needed, adjust the size of the feather stitch as you near the area where the sides join so two feather stitches are not on the same side of the basting line.

7 Use two strands of aqua wool and the feather stitch to work the outside line of the paisley. Work in the same manner as you did the yellow area.

8 Use two strands of orange red wool and the seed stitch to fill in the center area of the paisley.

9 Remove any remaining basting or tissue paper.

10 Use two strands of bead thread to attach the five pearls, using a single bead stitch and spacing them evenly along the right side of the pillow front. If using a striped fabric, place the beads in the center of a stripe on the right side. Sew through each bead twice to secure, and take two small stitches on the back of the fabric. Tie off thread. Repeat for the other beads.

11 Insert the pillow form. If necessary, stuff the pillow and sew the seam closed.

TOUCH OF GOLD FEDORA HAT

Crewel needlework can turn a classic hat into a fashion statement. This leaf and berry vine pattern is easy to work yet gives signature style to an otherwise ordinary accessory. White and metallic gold threads are striking against the gray felt. Switch it up with a lively color scheme to make a band for your favorite sun hat.

YOU WILL NEED

- ✖ fedora hat: black
- ✖ bamboo felt: lava rock
- ✖ fusible fleece
- ✖ stranded (three-ply) silk and wool blend: white
- ✖ single-strand 100 percent silk shimmer: gold
- ✖ fine braid, size 8: gold
- ✖ six-strand embroidery floss: medium old gold
- ✖ crewel and chenille needles
- ✖ sewing thread: dark and light gray
- ✖ permanent adhesive
- ✖ rotary cutter and cutting board
- ✖ pressing cloth
- ✖ quilter's chalk pencil or tailor's chalk in white

STITCHES USED

- ✖ straight
- ✖ fishbone
- ✖ French knot
- ✖ couching

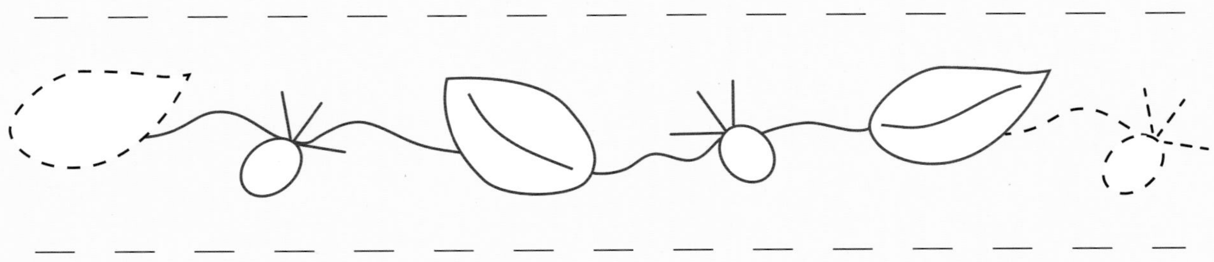

Touch of gold design pattern (actual size)

STITCHING INFORMATION

1 To determine the band length, measure around the base of the hat next to the brim and add 4" (10.2 cm).

2 Cut the piece of felt using the rotary cutter and cutting board. Recheck the band length to ensure it is long enough to crisscross over in the back of the hat.

3 Cut a piece of fusible fleece 1¼" (3.2 cm) wide and the same length as the band. Lay the piece of felt on a flat surface with the wrong side up. Place the piece of fleece, with the fusible side down, in the center of the wrong side of the felt band. Place the pressing cloth on top of the fleece, and fuse to the felt following the manufacturer's instructions. Fuse small sections at a time so the fleece does not slip out of place. Allow the felt band to cool.

4 Working from the back, fold the side pieces of felt over the fleece, and pin in place. Use the gray sewing thread to lace the two pieces together. The band should remain flat and not curl upward. (A)

XXXXXXXXXXXXXXXXXXXXXXXXXXXXXXXXXXXXXXXXXXXXXXXXX

5 Use the tissue basting method to transfer the pattern. The pattern is a repeat pattern. It is laid out so the dashed lines on the pattern will overlap what is already traced once you trace the initial pattern. This will give a straight pattern line across the area. Center the pattern on the tissue strip.

6 Center the tissue pattern on the front of the felt band. Baste the pattern using the light gray sewing thread.

7 Use one strand of the white silk/wool blend and the fishbone stitch to work the leaves. Place a straight compensating stitch at the tip of each leaf to start the fishbone.

8 Use the braid to work the French knots for the berries. Use a straight stitch for the three leaflets at the top of each berry. Work around the outside of the oval berry, and then fill in the center. Use a few sloppy knots with the regular French knots. (B)

C

9 Use the shimmer silk to work the laid thread along the basted line of the vine. Couch the laid thread down with one strand of the gold embroidery floss. The silk is a soft round thread, so it should remain round as you couch over it. Watch the tension on the couching thread. You can carry the laying thread on the back going over the leaf and berry backs. The laying thread should not be pulled snug. You will need to shape it to conform to the basting line.

10 Remove all basting thread. Use tweezers to remove any short stubborn pieces.

11 Place the band around the hat with the ends crisscrossed in the back. Gently pull the band snug. Slide a straight pin into the two pieces of felt to secure the ends together. Check to see if the band is still snug against the hat. Adjust if necessary and take a couple of basting stitches to hold the two pieces of band together. Do not pierce the hat. (C)

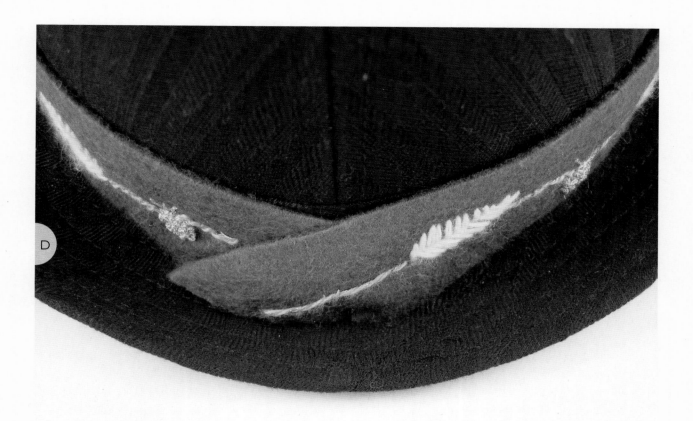

D

12 Remove the band from the hat, and trim the bottom piece of the band. Place the band back on the hat to check that enough of the bottom pieces has been trimmed away. Remove the hat and trim the top piece of felt. Place on the hat and check if additional trimming is necessary. **(D)**

13 Remove band from the hat and slip stitch the two pieces together along the cut edges, making sure your stitches do not show.

BASTING

For easy of removal of basting, be sure the basting stitches go all the way through the band to the back so the thread is visible.

CROSS-STITCH

XXXXXXXXXXXXXXXXXXXXXXXXXXXXXXX

Cross-stitch is counted embroidery following a charted pattern, most often worked with a basic X-shaped stitch. This technique is worked on even-weave fabric, counting each stitch and working uniform cross-stitches to create the design. It is easy to learn and will give you hours of pleasure creating projects for family and friends.

Before purchasing fabric for a pattern, choose the type of fabric and count size to determine the amount needed. Extra fabric is needed for finishing the project. Allow 2 to 3 inches (5 to 7.5 cm) on all sides for finishing. Before you start cross-stitching a project, finish the fabric edges by zigzag or serging or apply masking tape to the fabric edges to keep them from raveling.

WASHING

If it is necessary to clean a finished cross-stitch project, handwash in cool water using a mild soap or shampoo (dye free). Rinse well. Do not wring the fabric. Roll it in a towel to remove excess water. Smooth out on a flat surface to dry. While the fabric is still slightly damp, you can press the needlework by placing it face-down on a clean terry towel and using a pressing cloth.

cross-stitching with waste canvas (blue line)

Waste canvas is designed to be removed after it is stitched. This allows you to do counted cross-stitch on plain-weave fabric. You can embellish clothing, home décor items, linens, or whatever a needle and thread will stitch through. Mesh sizes are available in 6.5 to 16.

Use the directions shown here to work waste canvas projects. Try a few stitches on a piece of plain fabric using the canvas to see how the waste canvas works. This will let you know if you have made any stitching mistakes before working on the real project. Remember to keep an even tension.

1 Cut the piece of canvas larger than the finished design.

2 Find the center of the canvas and mark it with a permanent marker.

3 Find the center of the fabric and mark it with a straight pin. Place the marked canvas center over the fabric center, keeping the lines of the canvas straight across the fabric. Pin in place. Readjust as needed so the canvas lines are straight.

4 Baste the canvas to the fabric along the outer edges.

5 If using a lightweight fabric, use a non-fusible stabilizer (page 37) on the back of the fabric, basting it through the fabric and waste canvas. When the project is complete, trim away the excess stabilizer.

6 Work the design, centering it on the waste canvas. Work each stitch by going down and coming up into the middle of the corners that surround the square. Work each stitch so the thread touches the previously placed stitch or stitches in that corner. If the threads do not touch, you will end up with a small gap, showing the fabric between stitches. Take your time and place each stitch carefully.

7 When all stitching is completed, remove basting. Use a lightly dampened clean, lint-free cloth to gently sponge over the canvas. You can also use a clean spray bottle with a fine mist to lightly spray the area. Work carefully, barely dampening the threads. A word of caution: if the canvas becomes too moist, the threads will be more difficult to remove. Use a tweezers or your fingers to pull each thread up out of the stitching area.

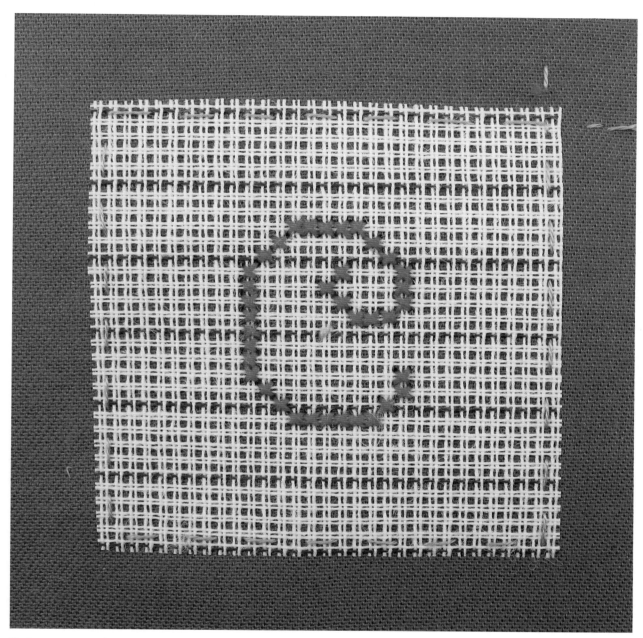

Waste canvas example

stitches

This section begins with the five basic stitches: the cross, quarter cross, half cross, three-quarter cross, and backstitch. The remaining stitches are counted decorative stitches or specialty stitches that will give you many new options.

HOW TO WORK CROSS-STITCH

Cross-stitch is worked following a pattern. The pattern is shown on a chart that is divided into squares. The key to cross-stitch charts is in understanding the cross-stitch square. A cross-stitch square represents the portion of the fabric to be covered by a cross-stitch. If you look at Aida even-weave fabric, you can easily see the fabric squares. The photo of a cross-stitch square shown here shows a simple cross-stitch worked over one square on Aida fabric. If working on linen, each cross-stitch would go over two threads unless indicated otherwise on the pattern. Symbols on the chart indicate where a cross-stitch is to be placed. Each unique symbol specifies a type and color of thread to use. Study the chart example and stitched example to understand how stitches are represented on the chart.

Design size is determined by the number of stitches and the fabric thread count (stitches per inch [cm]). You need to determine the count, both horizontal and vertical, to obtain the height and width of the fabric needed. To determine size, divide the number of stitches by the thread count. A design 32 stitches wide would be 2" (5.1 cm) wide on 16-count fabric and 4" (10.2 cm) wide on 8-count fabric.

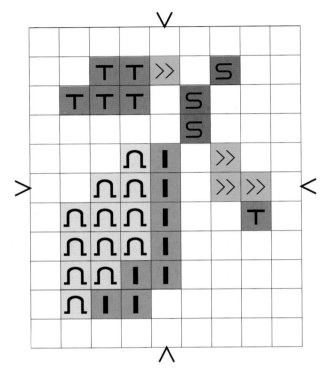

Chart example

Stitched example

Cross-stitch square

When centering the design and stitching the project, counting correctly is the most important concern. If you do not count up, down, or over correctly when starting to stitch or while stitching the design, it will not be worked correctly. Count and mark the spot with a straight pin, then count again to be sure it is correct. Patterns are marked with darker lines that run through the center area, or they have marks on the edge of the chart on all four sides to indicate the center. You may find it helpful to mark the horizontal and vertical center lines on the pattern with a highlighter.

Find the center of the fabric by using a ruler or carefully folding the fabric in half vertically, making sure the edges meet. Then, using your fingers, gently pinch the center folded area so

it leaves a slight mark. Open the fabric and fold it in half horizontally, repeating the marking process. Open the fabric and you should have a marked center. Baste along each of the creases, creating a marked center line on the fabric. If you are working on perforated paper, count both horizontally and vertically to find the center line of your paper. Baste the center lines with a light color sewing thread. A darker thread could bleed onto the paper.

For ease of counting, start stitching in the middle of the design. When working the stitches, don't carry the thread on the back for more than a stitch or two; rather, end the thread and start anew. Avoid using knots to begin or end your thread. Begin with a waste knot or away waste knot (page 42). Otherwise, leave a short tail on the back as you take the first stitch, and catch the tail under the next few stitches on the back of the fabric, securely burying the tail. End the thread by running it under the last few stitches worked.

For clarity, all of the stitches that follow are shown on an 8-count Aida. Decorative stitches work best on 14-count or higher linen fabric or Aida. When you are stitching on linen fabric, work over two threads for each square shown on the pattern.

The colored grid lines on the stitch graphs represent the threads in cross-stitch fabric; the white blocks represent the openings that the needle slides through to work the stitch.

CROSS

This stitch is worked from left to right as a single unit or in horizontal rows. Use the stab stitch or sewing method. Work the cross so all the top stitches slant in the same direction and use even tension. Avoid catching the thread of the previously placed stitch as you work the next cross.

You can use any type of thread for this stitch. Embroidery floss and over-dyed or hand-dyed floss work especially well.

Ways to use: home décor items, embellishment for clothing, monograms, pictorial scenes, filling

Also known as: Berlin, counted cross, point de marque cross-stitch

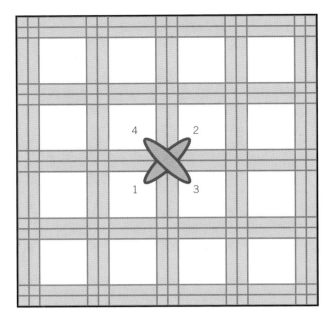

QUARTER CROSS

This partial stitch can be worked in any corner of the square. It is used to give the design a more realistic appearance. When working the quarter cross, it comes up at the corner of the square and goes down in the center fabric of the square. Use the stab stitch method, following the numbers and arrows on the graph.

You can use any type of thread for this stitch.

Ways to use: to add detail, round out outer edges of shapes

Also known as: partial cross

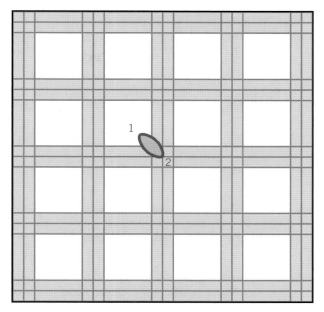

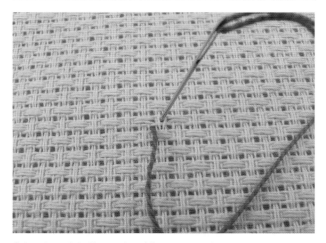

Going down into the center of the square

HALF CROSS

The half cross can be worked in either direction. It is always worked on the diagonal. These stitches are indicated on patterns by a colored diagonal line shown in the direction they are to be stitched. The color key will also indicate the color to use. Use the stab stitch method or sewing method.

The half cross can also be used to work a border around the pattern. Work one row with the diagonals going to the right and the next row with the diagonals going to the left. Repeat the row of diagonals going to the right to create a border of three rows. Each of these rows can be stitched in a different color, or work all the rows in the same color.

You can use any type of thread for this stitch. Twisted or hand-dyed single-strands threads work especially well.

Ways to use: lacy affects, background, bands

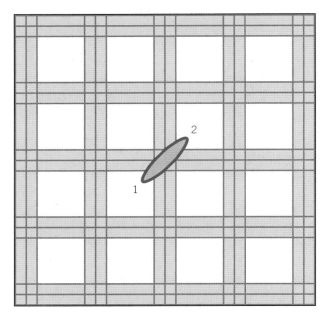

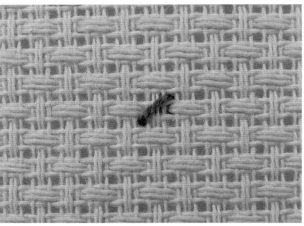

THREE-QUARTER CROSS

The three-quarter stitch can be worked in any direction. Work the first half of the cross-stitch; then come up as if you were placing the second half, but take the thread under the previous half stitch and down into the center of the square.

These stitches are usually indicated on the pattern by colored diagonal lines with the short stitches going in the direction they are to be stitched. The color key will list them in the color to be used. Use the stab stitch method, following the numbers and arrows on the graph.

Stranded threads or single-strand threads work best.

Ways to use: add rounded appearance, detail

Also known as: partial cross

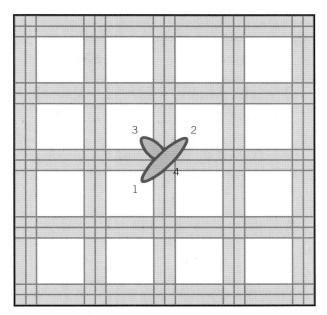

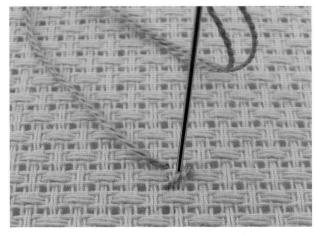

Going down into the center of the square under half cross

BACKSTITCH

This stitch can be worked in any direction. The backstitch will be indicated by a straight colored line on the pattern where it is to be stitched. The color key will show the color to be used. Use the stab stitch method, following the numbers and arrows on the graph. Backstitches add depth to areas in the design. The pattern will indicate the number of strands to use.

Backstitch is often used to achieve the desired effect rather than half or quarter stitches.

You can use any type of thread for this stitch.

Ways to use: outline shapes, define areas, borders

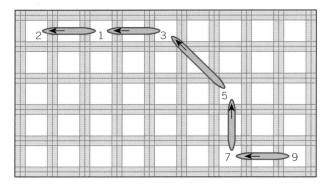

SMYRNA CROSS

This stitch is worked from left to right, right to left or vertically. This versatile stitch is a combination of two cross-stitches. The size of the stitch can be changed to fit the area. It is shown stitched over four threads. It can also be stitched over two, six, or eight threads. For a border area, alternate the over two threads and over four threads sizes of this stitch across the area.

You can use any type of thread. Hand-dyed single strand threads work well for this stitch.

Ways to use: borders, bands, filling

Also known as: Leviathan, railway, double cross, straight cross

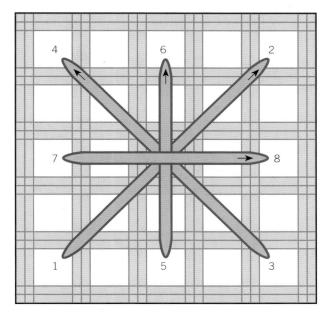

DIAMOND EYELET

This stitch is worked from right to left. For best results, work the stitches as shown on the graph so you will be going down into a dirty hole, not coming up through a dirty hole. This stitch gives a lacy look when worked over a large area or worked as a border stitch.

You can use any type of thread for this stitch. Hand-dyed single strand thread or metallic braid work especially well.

Ways to use: stars, bands

Also known as: star eyelet

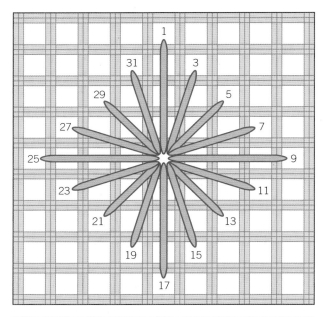

DAISY MOTIF

This sweet motif is a variation of a lazy daisy. This stitch can we worked in any direction. As you work the stitch, you'll need to use your finger to hold the left side of the loop in place while you complete the tie-down stitch. Watch the tension on this stitch, as it is easy to pull it too snug. When the motif is complete, check to be sure it lies flat against the fabric with no puckering of the fabric.

You can use any type of thread for this stitch.

Ways to use: bands, borders, filling

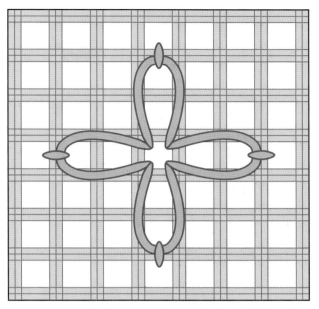

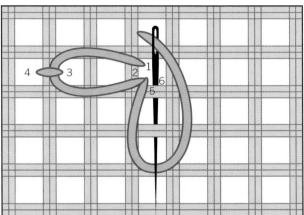

Creating the loop

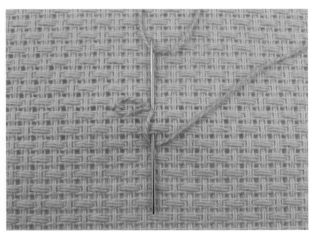

Pulling thread through

VIOLET BLOSSOMS CANDLE BAND

Fields of wild violets blooming are a wonder to behold. These stitched violets will add a touch of beauty to your home for guests and family to enjoy.

STITCHING INSTRUCTIONS

1 Baste center line on Stitchband.

2 Stitch design using center line as a guide.

3 Remove center basting thread.

4 Trim ends of band as needed for a straight edge.

5 Fold under one end of the Stitchband ¼" (0.6 cm). Use ecru sewing thread to sew raw edge to the back of the band. Stitches should not go through the fabric to the front.

6 Measure the circumference of the candle. Create a circle the size of the circumference by overlapping the sewn edge of the Stitchband on the outside of the circle until measurement is reached. Pin layers together. Sew the two pieces together along the folded edge of the top piece.

7 Trim loose band as needed and slide band on candle. The band can be positioned in the center of the candle or placed at the bottom of the candle.

Never leave burning candles unattended.

YOU WILL NEED

- ✶ 16 count Stitchband length of the circumference of the candle plus three inches (7.6 cm)
- ✶ six- strand embroidery floss: light forest green, lemon, light blue violet, light avocado green, light parrot green, dark forest green, forest green, dark grey green, very light golden yellow, cornflower blue
- ✶ tapestry needle
- ✶ sewing thread to match banding
- ✶ candle

STITCHES USED

- ✶ cross
- ✶ Smyrna
- ✶ backstitch

STITCH COUNT (EXCLUDES BORDER)

- ✶ 41" W × 28" H (104 × 71 cm)

STITCH DESIGN

- ✶ centered on band
- ✶ baste the center lines

APPROXIMATE FINISHED SIZE

- ✶ will depend on candle size

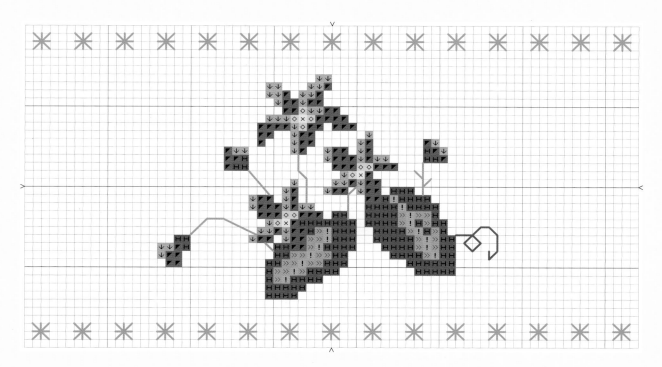

VIOLET BLOSSOMS CHART

H	987	dark forest green
>>	989	forest green
↓	341	light blue violet
◤	3807	cornflower blue
◇	307	lemon
!	164	light forest green
×	3078	very light golden yellow
——	470	light avocado green (stem)
——	3051	dark grey green (tendril)
——	907	light parrot green (smyrna)

COLOR KEY

Smyrna stitch: 2 strands

Cross-stitch: 2 strands

Backstitch stem and tendril: 1 strand

SPRINGTIME JOURNAL

Spring brings beautiful color with sweet smells from all the blooming flowers. This posy will call forth thoughts of spring as you write in your "Go Green" journal with its handmade paper and hemp cover.

STITCHING INFORMATION

1 Baste center line on paper.

2 Stitch design using center line as a guide. (A)

3 Remove center basting thread.

4 Trim the perforated paper to within one row of the stitching.

5 Use the rotary cutter and cutting board to cut a piece of the brown cardstock ⅛" (3 mm) larger on all four sides than the stitched work. Cut the red cardstock ⅛" (3 mm) larger on all four sides than the brown cardstock.

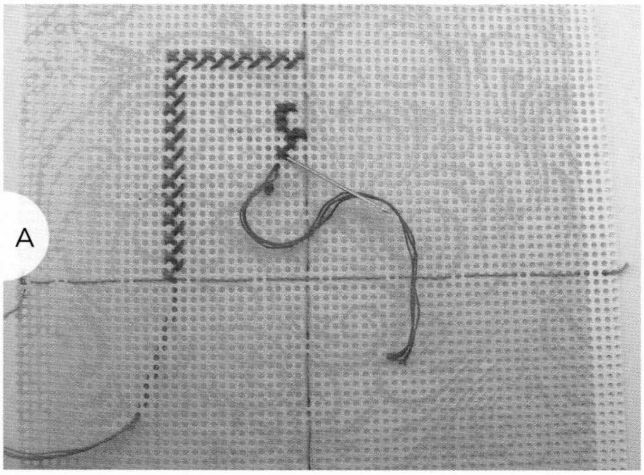

YOU WILL NEED

- 5" × 7¼" (12.7 × 18.4 cm) natural hemp handmade journal
- 4½" × 6" (11.4 × 15.2 cm) piece of 14-count perforated paper: pale gray green
- six-strand embroidery floss: medium light moss green, black, dark coral, coral, avocado green, very light topaz, and black avocado green
- tapestry needle, size 24
- rotary cutter and cutting board
- cardstock paper: dark mocha brown and bright orange red
- permanent adhesive

STITCHES USED

- cross
- backstitch

STITCH COUNT

- 31" W × 49" H (78.7 × 124.5 cm)

STITCH DESIGN

- centered on paper
- baste the center lines

APPROXIMATE FINISHED SIZE (PERFORATED PAPER)

- 2¼" × 3½" (5.7 × 8.9 cm)

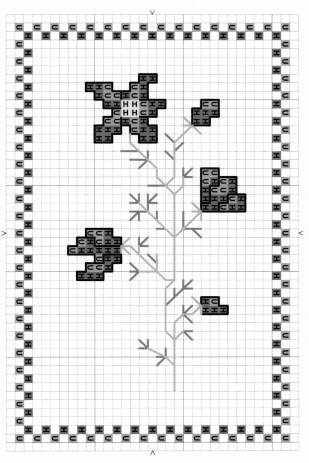

6 Use the permanent adhesive to glue the needlework to the brown cardstock. Using a toothpick, place permanent adhesive on the back of the stitched work along the back of the cross-stitches and on each flower. Glue to the center of the front of the brown cardstock.

7 Place permanent adhesive on the front side of the red cardstock and glue it the back of the brown cardstock. Glue the back of the red cardstock to the front of the journal. Refer to the photograph for placement, or chose your own location on the journal front.

SPRINGTIME JOURNAL CHART

⚏	34	coral dark
⊏	35	coral
H	72	topaz very light
▬	310	black
▬	934	black avocado green
▬	166	moss green medium light
▬	469	avocado green

COLOR KEY

Cross-stitch: 3 strands

Backstitch flowers and petals: 1 strand

Backstitch main stem, branches, and leaves: 3 strands

glossary

Here are the meanings of some of the common terms and phrases used for needlework:

Bead embroidery stitches. Adding beads within an embroidery stitch to enhance it.

Bead stitches. Beads stitched on fabric using a beading thread.

Even-weave fabric. Cloth in which the number of warp (vertical) threads equals the number of weft (horizontal) threads in a square inch.

Plain-weave fabric. An over-under motion is used to weave the fabric without a definite thread count.

Rhythm. How the needle goes through the canvas/thread to complete the stitch.

Sewing method. To stitch by sliding the needle in and out of the fabric on the front side of the fabric in one motion.

Snug. To pull a thread secure against the fabric or canvas.

Stab-stitch method. To stitch by moving the needle up through the fabric or canvas and down through the fabric or canvas in two motions.

Strand (ply). A single thread as it comes from the skein or spool. An individual thread separated from a stranded thread. A single strand is sometimes referred to as a ply.

Taut. To keep the stitching thread or canvas mesh firm to the touch.

Travel or traveling. The path or direction the stitch will cover.

Stitch path. The area where the stitches are to be placed.

Unit or stitch unit. A stitch unit is a completed stitch pattern. It can be comprised of several stitches or a single stitch.

about the author

Linda Wyszynski lives with her husband Dennis in Mount Pleasant, South Carolina and is the owner of Hearthside Creations, LLC. She is a professional needle arts designer who has over twenty years' experience as an artist creating freelance needlework projects for publication. She began her designing career painting custom needlepoint canvases for local needlepoint shops in Minneapolis. She is an author of needlework textbooks, magazine articles, and multi-author books. Her work can be seen on the newsstands in craft, needlework, and home décor magazines.

Linda has always been active in the art and needlework community including the following: CHA Designer Section Council, Board of Directors Society of Craft Designers, and Outreach After School Project program for a local EGA Chapter, Board of Directors Needlework Guild of Minnesota, Twin Cities Metropolitan Art Council Board, and Polk County NC Community Arts Council Committee.

She is passionate about needlework and continues to be active in both local needlework chapters and national organizations. She is currently a member of the Embroiderers' Guild of America (EGA), American Needlepoint Guild (ANG), the National Needlework Association (TNNA), and the Craft and Hobby Association (CHA).

index

the first time series

THE ABSOLUTE BEGINNER'S GUIDES

There's a first time for everything. Enjoy the journey
and achieve success with the First Time series!

LEARN BY
DOING
• • •
STEP-BY-STEP
BASICS
+
PROJECTS

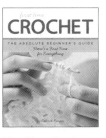

First Time Knitting

978-1-58923-805-3

First Time Crochet

978-1-58923-825-1

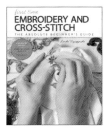

First Time Quilting

978-1-58923-824-4

*First Time Embroidery and
Cross-Stitch*

978-1-63159-797-8

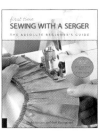

First Time Sewing

978-1-58923-804-6

First Time Sewing with a Serger

978-1-63159-714-5

First Time Window Treatments

978-1-63159-785-5

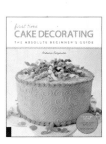

First Time Garment Fitting

978-1-58923-962-3

First Time Cake Decorating

978-1-58923-961-6

First Time Jewelry Making

978-1-63159-698-8

First Time Felting

978-1-63159-803-6

128 pages | Paperback | Creative Publishing international QUARRY